'FOLLOW ANY STREAM'

by George Birtill, O.B.E., J.P.

Published by Nelson Brothers Printers,
Fellery Street, Chorley, Lancashire

First Published 1968 by Guardian Press, Chorley
and Reprinted 1972

Second Reprint 1976
Third Reprint 1980
by Nelson Brothers Printers, Chorley

1

FOREWORD

WHEN I got lost on a school outing to the country the master told me afterwards, "You can always find your way in the country. Just follow a stream."

"What stream?" I asked.

"Any stream," he answered.

After that I noticed that if you ever came to a village there was always a stream nearby. This is specially true of the country drained by the Yarrow and the Douglas with which this series will largely deal.

The Author.

ACKNOWLEDGEMENTS

Victoria County History of Lancashire.

Baines's History of Lancashire.

Topography of Preston (Mannex).

The Rev. W. G. Procter, 'Ancient Parish of Croston' (Lancashire and Cheshire Historical Society, 1908).

'Croston Church', Rev. R. A. Rawstorne.

The personal recollections of many residents.

also R. Sharpe-France, Esq., County Archivist.

and R. H. Blackburn, Esq., Chorley Borough Librarian and his staff.

CHAPTER ONE

ULF THE VIKING LIKED IT HERE

ULNES WALTON has always been something of a Shibboleth Local pronunciation is "Oos Warton' the 'N' being being silent, probably because it should never have been there.

Strangers just stare in astonishment the first time they hear it. Once during a long session in court a barrister who had skilfully produced 47 witnesses asked the forty-eighth where she lived. When she told him "Oos Warton' he put his thumbs in the pockets of his waistcoat and said owlishly — "Yes Indeed."

For me Ulnes Walton has never really been a tongue twister. At a very early age, I was told that a Viking called Ulf sailed up the River Lostock on the incoming tide. When he got as far as Littlewood where the tide stops, he tied up his boat.

What he saw pleased him so much that he decided to settle. He cut down the trees of Littlewood which was then rather large, and built a wall for his protection. Thus was created Ulf's Wall Town.

There is no proof in history for this derivation, but the Viking called Ulf a tall man with a shaggy red beard and piercing blue eyes, who had a voice like thunder, has been real enough to me since I first heard about him.

In fact when I first went inside the old barn at Littlewood and saw the massive oak timbers, which support the roof I had the impression that this indeed was the work of ship builders. With its ribs and cross members it did look rather like an inverted ship, such as the Vikings would use.

The barn is old of course, but not that old. It has a base of dressed red sandstone, and is probably sixteenth century. It is constructed of oak beams once filled in with lath and plaster, which makes it very similar to the old barn at Worden. This hints at the work of the Farington's who held Littlewood as far back as 1505 — and indeed still own the present farm.

BEFORE CONQUEST

So far as the Walton's are concerned, the earliest known member was Ulf de Walton who was living about 1160, but this was after the Norman Conquest when the family may have been displaced. After all they were there first!

Anyhow, the family prospered under their Norman masters and ultimately Master Adam Walton, who was Precentor at Lichfield Cathedral, inherited the family manors and estates in Ulnes Walton, Eccleston, Leyland and Hoole. He died in 1306.

The barn at Littlewood. Ridley-lane which runs past the farm used to lead to Cocker Bar and Nixon-lane, but the R.O.F. depot got between.

Bullen's Farm. The name is probably older than the building. It was the old spelling of Boleyn.

When the male line ran out, Maud de Walton, wife of William de Bracebridge, succeeded, but in 1347 she and her husband granted the manor of Ulnes Walton and moieties of Eccleston, Heskin and Leyland to Henry, Earl of Lancaster in exchange for Barley in Yorkshire.

Whatever happened to the property, the manor courts were held at Littlwood and it seems that some of the penalties were carried out there too.

For 1504 for instance, it is recorded that a 'ducking stool' (a kind of seesaw used for ducking people in a pond) was out of repair. In 1578 it was ordered that the banks of the Lostock should be kept clear of trees and other undergrowth so that the river should be kept three yards wide.

All this would seem to suggest that the original settlement in Ulnes Walton was at Littlewood. On the other hand, the part known as the town is in Ulnes Walton-lane, within a stone's throw of Leyland St. James's Church. A number of cottages are still called Town Cottages and one of them used to be known as the Town Hall. Nearby there was also a penfold for collection stray animals.

There is no clock on the 'town hall'. They don't need one it seems, for one lady who has resided hereabouts for sixty years, assured me that on a sunny day, you can read the figures on the clock of Leyland Parish Church!

The country is so flat down here that the square tower of the church stands out on the hill like a castle. It is a view that seems to whisk one back into earlier days when knights and their ladies rode along on fine horses.

At any rate there are a number of interesting old farm houses on either side, which suggests the lane is very old. Most of them are not ashamed of their age and shout out the date like Norris's for instance, where it is 1755.

It is to this century that the older ones seem to belong, but one can have other ideas about Bullen's Farm which stands not far from Lostock Brow.

OLD NAME

The building, low beamed and picturesque, probably dates from the reign of Queen Anne. A broken date stone found near bears the initials I with R and H below the date 1708.

The name however, is older than the building for it is the way they used to spell Boleyn. This might not seem important, except that Sir Henry Farington who held land in these parts, was knighted at the coronation of Anne Boleyn in 1533.

Also he and the Earl of Derby reported the priest at Croston for slandering that lady. Maybe there was a reason in all this to christen a farm Bullen.

Sir Henry, of course, a personality at court. He had been one of the four squires who kept the door of the King's Bedchamber in the reign of Henry VII. Later as a 'Knight of the King's Body' he had the duty of seeing that tenants of manors wore 'no badge cognisance or livery, but the Red Rose'.

After the Wars of the Roses the King was determined to wipe out private armies. In seeing that rule was obeyed, Sir Henry was acting directly on behalf of the King.

Becconsal Chapel House – Probably an endowment of the Chapel of Becconsall.

Now the centre of Mr. Martin Kevill's Museum, Gradwell's, a lovely farmhouse, built on the site of an older mansion.

He performed similar service for Henry VIII, which may show his cercern for Ann Boleyn. That the name remains after she had been beheaded could mean personal regard for the lady, rather than loyalty to the King.

Concern

CHIEF JUSTICE

Another courtier who must have ridden down here was Sir Anthony Browne, Chief Justice of Common Pleas to Mary Tudor. Sir Henry knew him well. He must have done, Sir Anthony was the third husband of his granddaughter Joan, for whom he broke the entail of the family lands in Farington, with the result that through her daughter they went to the Huddletons.

Although Sir Henry had good reasons for cutting out a younger son, the Bownes are suspected of having used pressure on the ageing knight.

Sir Anthony was a zealous Catholic, but did not hesitate to make money out of the confiscation of religious property. In fairness, it should be mentioned he was in other land deals for the crown.

In the reign of Edward VI in 1551, he acquired the manor of Ulnes Walton after it had been disposed of by the Waltons it descended with the earldom and the dutchy of Lancaster, now the royal house, and was disposed of by the King, who was hard-up as was usual in those days.

Eight years later Sir Anthony sold half of the manor to Sir Thomas Gerrard and half to William Farington. William was not affected by the jiggery pokery work at Farington. The son by a second marriage, he had been given Worden for his estate. This may explain why he was on good terms with Sir Anthony who in fact nominated him in 1555 for the Middle Temple.

William's legal training stood him in good stead, for he became steward to three earls of Derby. He must have ridden down here—and pretty frequently too—on his way to Lathom across Hoscar Moss.

The Derby connection may explain why there was no bidding from William when his friend Sir Thomas Gerrard sold the second half of Ulnes Walton manor to the Earl of Derby in 1562.

CHAPEL HOUSE

Later his half of the manor went to Sir Richard Molyneux. Holding land from his family was Humphrey Marsh who died in 1628. This family appeared to have given their name to Marsh House, which is beyond the Lostock.

Alongside Marsh House is the drive to Becconsall Chapel House—a reminder that Becconsall now linked with Hesketh, was part of Croston Parish.

The separation occurred in 1821.

That the house is so far from the chapel means that it was probably part of the endowment which provided the stipend for the clergy.

Lostock Brow, Holker Brook noisily meets the Lostock here. The bridge replaced a wooden one in 1937. Pictured from Holker-lane.

Town cottages in Ulnes Walton-lane. Cottages on the Southport-road are called New Town.

11

There is another straw in the wind. Joan Farrington's second husband was Charles Becconsall, by whom she had Dorothy, successor to Farrington. Perhaps Joan or Dorothy gave some Ulnes Walton land to the chapel.

Another family who made their mark in Ulnes Walton was the Gradwells. The estate on Barber's Moor not far from the head of Ulnes Walton-lane, was left to William Gradwell by John Charnock of Farington in 1571.

The Gradwells like the Charnocks were zealous Catholics, and when Elizabeth started to penalise people who did not conform, they were amongst the first to be fined. Their names appeared regularly on the recusancy lists until the reign ⸱ of James II.

According to Gillow's Dictionary of English Catholics "They supplied the church with several virtuous and learned priests during the days of persecution and throughout the whole of that period maintained the chaplain at their house at Barble's (Barber's) Moor."

This may have given rise to the idea that once Gradwell's was the site of a monastic house. This was not the case. There was however, a mansion on the site for the hearth tax rolls of 1666 in the reign of Charles II, shows Gradwells as the largest house in the district. This has gone however, so has the chapel.

MUSEUM

Out of the remains the present Gradwell's was built about 1700 and the initials of William Gradwell are preserved in the brickwork. It forms a delightful centre for Mr. Martin Kevill's transport museum.

The presence of the cross in the garden has produced the legend that it marks the burial place of a monk. A servant girl is said to have fallen in love with him and drowned herself in the 40ft. deep well near the house.

Gillow records, however, that a corner of the garden was once used as a burial ground. The cross which can still be seen originally covered the remains of the Rev. William Winckley who died in 1740.

His aunt was the wife of Christopher Gradwell. There was also a Rev. Christopher Gradwell, who served as a priest at Sheffield for 22 years. When he died in 1758 the male line became extinct.

The Sarcow Lady is also supposed to have haunted this spot. but she really belongs to Croston, for the main road is the boundary!

Perhaps because it is on the Southport main road, this part of Ulnes Walton, particularly the bit near Mayor's timber yard, is the most widely known. The cottages and the Rose and Crown Inn have the aspects of a pretty village. As a matter of fact, before William Mayor starting his bobbin turning in the midle of the last century, there was a windmill, where the saw mill now stands.

This probably one of a number in these parts, which receive plenty of breezes from the sea!

There were water mills too powered by the Lostock. Two were mentioned in 1616.

The other principal road through Ulnes Walton is Leyland-lane from Roe Moor. It gives pleasant views of countryside which is still unspoiled.

Near the junction of Flag-lane and Holker-lane is Balshaw Farm and a number of cottages named after a smithy. There is not much doubt that the one near Balshaw's Farm last served this purpose, but replaced the one at the corner of Holker-lane which is shown in 1846 as Porter's Smithy!

Holker-lane by the way is named after the Holker Brook that joins the Lostock at Lostock Brow in Ulnes Walton-lane.

Follow any stream — and you get back where you started from — almost!

CHAPTER TWO

MEETING OF THE WATERS

WYMOTT BROOK, Bretherton's north boundary, joins the Lostock just above Lostock Bridge on the Bretherton road, about 100 yards from Croston Railway Station. Wymott is from Old English meaning river mouth or a confluence of waters. It could be used again in this bit of country, for a mile downstream the Lostock joins the Yarrow, and then three-quarters of a mile further on the Yarrow joins the Douglas. Truly a meeting of the waters!

According to a map 120 years old, the Douglas is navigable up to this point for ships not exceeding 30 tons. This refers to the new course which is straight like a canal. Water still flows, however, along the old course, which for some distance is part of the canal. It also forms Bretherton's western boundary.

The rivers old and new meet just above Tarleton Bridge, where the Liverpool road crosses both river and canal. In fact, most people think of this district as Tarleton, but east of the river is Bank, once the home of the Banastres of Bank, a family who go back in records to 1200.

Henry Banastre of Bank died in 1526, possessed of Bank and other properties in Bretherton, Tarleton, Becconsall and Hesketh. Another Henry Banastre, who was buried at Croston in 1665, was killed in Cheshire by a Manxman called Colcloth.

He was succeeded by his brother Christopher, who was High Sheriff from 1669-70. On his death in 1690 the male line ran out. The estate went to daughters Anne, wife of Thomas Fleetwood, and Elizabeth, who married Robert Parker, ancestor of the Cuerden family.

Daughter of Thomas and Anne, Henrietta Maria Fleetwood, married Thomas Legh, son of Sir Richard Legh, of Lyme. Thomas, who made his home at Bank, was M.P. for Newton-in-Makerfield from 1698 to 1710. In this way the estate descended to Lord Lilford.

Bretherton derives from Brotherton, meaning a joint ownership of brothers, and it may be significant that half of the manor was held by another branch of the Banastres, of whom Sir Thomas, elected K.G. in 1373, was a member. He was lost at sea and his son Edward died three years later, leaving a daughter Constance as heir. The result was that the estate was split up and half came into possession of Sir Gilbert Gerrard, Master of Rolls to Queen Elizabeth I.

The subdivisions were acquired by the Heskeths of Rufford at the beginning of the nineteenth century, and sold to Lord Lilford in 1880, uniting the entire manor.

Bank Hall, viewed through the trees on a summer evening.

Carr House, a warm and cheerful place, now a Dolls' Museum.

CLOCK TOWER

Bank Hall itself dates back to 1608, but it was restored and enlarged in 1832-33. The tower, with its clock on the south face is a distinguishing feature of the hall, which is built of brick.

Not far from Bank Hall, on the Liverpool Road, is a windmill, which has been converted into a house. This bears the date 1741, but mention of a windmill at Bank occurs in records for 1526, and this would probably be on the same site.

When Henry Banastre died in London in June, 1641, it was recorded that he held Bank of the King and "a windmill in Bretherton" with other lands in a dozen neighbouring townships.

Further north along the Liverpool Road, is the junction with Carr House Lane, and on the corner a bungalow which was once a toll house. The lane gets its name from the gracious three storey building of warm red brick, which stands back from the road.

This seventeenth century house is as cheerful inside as out, as many thousands have discovered when visiting Mr. Barry Elder's doll museum which is housed there. Mr. Elder has also turned his attention to the gardens where 1,200 rose trees have been planted.

From early boyhood. I have always known this building as Jeremiah Horrocks's House. On the first floor the middle room which is larger than the others because of the recessed window over the porch is said to be where Horrocks made his observation of the transit of Venus on November 24th, 1639.

One version infers that he was only able to make the observation after he had carried out his Sunday duties at Hoole Church, where he was assisting. He was, however, only twenty years of age, which was too young for a curate, and it is thought that if he was staying at Carr House at all, it would be as family tutor. In that event, he would hardly occupy the best room on the first floor,.

At any rate, his calculations which predicted Venus crossing the sun's disc were the beginning of English astronomy, and justify the Chapel at Hoole Church, and other memorials to the brilliant young man, who died little over a year later on January 3rd, 1641.

Carr House was built for Mr. John Stones by his two brothers who seem to have done very well in business. The large headstone over the door carries the inscription "Thomas Stones of London haberdasher and Andrewe Stones of Amsterdam merchant have builded this house of their own charges and giveath the same unto their brother John Stones: Ano Domini 1613 laus."

'LOST' HAMLET

Which ever way one approaches Bretherton village, the road twists and turns in an incredible manner. From Croston, the first building to arouse curiosity is a gable fronted farm on the left, with a semi-circular window on

This house of unusual appearance has an unusual name.
It is called Over Hall.

Known as Church House this farm was built in the seventeenth century. The date and the names of John and Mary Hesketh, for whom it was built, appear in stone over the door.

the third floor. This house has the name of "Over Hall," which is supposed to relate to its use for keeping a watch on the surrounding countryside. Certainly the view from the top window is very extensive.

Locally, the district is still referred to as Thorpe, the name of a hamlet which was acquired by Sir Thomas Banastre in 1369 and according to some authorities, to have become submerged in the rest of the estate. Whether it has thus disappeared or not, Thorpe had the distinction of being the only vill in Leyland Hundred to be held of the King in chief. It was sublet in 1212 by Richard de Freckleton to a family named Thorpe who held it for 150 years.

Bretherton had a school very early. It was founded in 1653 by James Fletcher, a London merchant born at Bretherton. He purchased part of the confiscated estates of James the seventh Earl of Derby who was beheaded at Bolton for his part in the Civil War.

The old schoolhouse is still there, and over the door is the following inscription: "This free schoole was erected and built at the proper costs; and charges of James Fletcher of London merchant: and at the request of Mistris Jane Fletcher his wife who was born in this town in the fourteenth: Onni doni, 1653."

Over the doorway of a picturesque farm house, opposite the school, is a stone inscribed with the names John and Mary Hesketh and the date 1698. Tradition has it that the house was built for a daughter of James Fletcher on her marriage to a Hesketh. The building is better known as "Church House" however, which suggests other possibilities.

Although the Parish Church of St. John the Baptist was only built in 1840, the Order of St. John of Jerusalem purchased land in the village, and a Charter of 1344 records that a chapel had been "recently built." A pathway past the church is called Church Lane to this day and a regular copse of trees in the fields nearby has caused speculation that this might be the site of the chapel.

The present church is a pleasant building of stone and when the chancel was added in 1909, the old pews were used to panel the walls which had produced a pleasing effect.

In the chancel there is a fine oak reredos in memory of the Rev. Robert Gardiner, who was rector for almost fifty years, and a "Mary Window" given by the rector's wife, Mr. Gardiner and friends.

For its size, Bretherton is remarkable for having a Methodist Chapel built in 1824 and rebuilt in 1836 and 1883, and a Congregational Chapel once called Ebenezer, built in 1819 and replaced by the present building in 1896.

The Roman Catholics, as in many villages, worshipped in farm-houses, and associated with this Martinside Farm which is quite close to the parish church. A date stone for 1718 carries the initial 'H' with 'H' and 'E' beneath.

EYES LANE

At the end of the village, where one turns sharp right for Carr House Lane, most people are intrigued by the name of Eyes Lane on the left. This spelling is a mistake. The south-west half of Bretherton had been known for a considerable time as 'Ees."

Philogists have no explanation to offer for this, but at a shrewd guess I should say it is Lancashire for "His", which is the equivalent of the Irish "Himself".

Who was "Himself" in these parts, may be a matter for conjecture.

Reclaiming of the local marshes was sanctioned by Act of Parliament in 1800 and anyone who follows Eyes Lane to the River Douglas, where it is crossed by Red Bridge, must be struck by a draining that has gone on, and is going on still. In fact, the river had been banked up so that the water level is now highter than the surrounding land and the general impression is of the fen country or Holland.

Now a home—the windmill at Banks.

The old school house at Bretherton is another building which, like Carr House, carries its story carved on a large slab over the entrance.

The River Yarrow joins the Douglas here. This view is from Red Bridge. In the distance is Isle of Man Farm.

CHAPTER THREE

A VILLAGE IN SAXON TIMES

Even those who have passed but once recall Croston as a place with a hump-back bridge, a cross, a narrow street and a square towered church. This is a glimpse which is not easily forgotten. It somehow links the village with long ago.

Town Bridge is a striking specimen of its kind, built in 1672 at the cost of under £30, but still carries the weight of quite heavy vehicles. It is scheduled as a structure of historical interest.

Other bridges have interesting names, like Fishery Bridge at the end of Westhead Road, and the two handing bridges in Meadow Lane, which was once a turnpike road. Great Hanging Bridge crosses the new course of the River Douglas and Little Hanging Bridge the old one. The old course of the River Yarrow joins the two just above where they meet, and forms a triangle known as Isle of Man, from which the nearby farm gets its name.

As one looks out across this country now green with crops, it is hard to believe that this was once marsh and mere and perhaps the scene of desperate battles long ago.

Yet there is a claim that this River Douglas is the Douglas in Linuis upon which King Arthur fought one of his twelve battles against the Saxons.

Whether or not the battle was as mythical as some authorities say King Arthur was, the indications point to Croston having a castle in very early times. The name Castle Walks still persists and this derives from Castle Walls. In the absence of the unual masonry found near ruined castles, it is fair to assume that this one was made of wood – the type the Saxons built. If this was the case the last place to be subdued after the battle.

This leads to interesting speculation on how Croston may have got the cross from which it is named. King Arthur and his Britons were Christians. In one battle, King Arthur is said to have borne the image of the Holy Virgin on his shoulders and "with the power of the Lord Jesus and Mary" to have put the Saxons to flight. The Saxons of course worshipped warlike gods and their conception of heaven was Wodan's Hall where they reposed on couches, drinking unlimited quantities of ale, from the skulls of enemies killed in battle.

What more likely place for the Christian warrior to place the cross of victory, than near the castle where the pagan enemies had been holding out. This would make Croston's name as old as the Sixth Century of Christianity.

RELIGIOUS CENTRE

The popular explanation for the name, which is Engilsh in origin, is that in time of Paulinus who converted the North of England at the instigation of Pope Gregory the Great, a monk came to the marshland and stuck his sharp pointed wooden cross at what appeared to be a good centre. Perhaps he chose the bank of the River Yarrow, so that converts could be baptised in its waters. He may even have used the spring which is at the base of the present cross and within living memory was the site of the parish pump.

Whichever version one believes, this makes the name very old, for Paulinus who was first Archbishop of York died in 644.

Another indication that Croston was one of the earliest religious centres is the extensive area of the original parish. It included the now separate parishes of Hoole (separated in 1642) Rufford, Tarleton, Hesketh Bank, Mawdesley with Bispham, Bretherton and of course, Chorley, which was detached anyway by Leyland and Eccleston in between.

This must have made it a very valuable possession and after the conquest, the Norman Count Roger of Poictu no doubt thought he was doing himself spiritual good when he granted it to the Abbey of St. Martin in Sees. The Prior and Convent of Lancaster presented the rectors until Edward the Third, during the war with France, claimed Lancaster for himself as an alien priory.

Over the Pack Horse Bridge, the square tower of the church.

22

Church Street with the cross at one end and the church at the other. The Parish pump once stood in front of the base of the cross.

Croston remained in the hands of the Crown until Henry the Seventh granted it to his new monastery of Syon near London in 1420.

In the circumstances it is not surprising that one of the priests who expressed himself in strong terms about the intention of Henry the Eighth to marry Anne Boleyn was sent to London and did not return.

The suppression of religious houses seems to have changed the patronage again and the rector in 1557, one Thomas Leeming, was presented by Sir Anthony Brown, a trafficier in confiscated property.

The previous incumbent, Thomas Bond, had served for 31 years, through the changes imposed by Henry the Eighth, Edward the Sixth and Mary Tudor. It has been suggested he was for this reason, a version of the "Vicar of Bray", but parish clergy in these times put their pastoral duties first and were accommodating where doctrine was concerned.

THE CHANTRIES

Possibly the biggest disturbance in the parish was not so much the Reformation itself, as the closing of the chantries early in the reign of Edward the Sixth.

Croston church itself had four regularly endowed known by the names of the proprietors Beconshaw, Hesketh, Ashton and Banastre. When the endowments were confiscated, the clergy were turned adrift, deprived of their subsistence. This reduced the numbers in Croston Parish from 12 in 1547 to two in 1565.

It was during the Commonwealth that Croston probably lost its cross. Mr. James Hyett was appointed rector by Charles the First, but he in 1646 became a Puritan of the narrowest sort, signing the "Harmonius Consent" which defined toleration as "putting a sword in a madman's hand, a cup of poison in the hands of a child."

On "Black Bartholomew's" Day in August 1662, he was one of the clergy expelled for refusing to resume use of the Book of Common Prayer and other provisions of the Act of Uniformity. His feelings against the prayer book were so strong that he left instructions in his will that he was to be buried without it. To this proviso his successor at Croston, James Pilkington B.D., might have objected, particularly as he was the son of a royalist mayor of Wigan. However when Mr. Hyett died only six months later, the new rector not only gave permission for the funeral but waived his right to officiate. The service (without the prayer book) was taken by Mr. Welch who had also been expelled at Chorley, where he was known as "a Godlie painfull preaching minister."

SCHOOL FOUNDER

That James Pilkington should behave in this manner, must be a measure of the esteem in which Mr. Hyett was held in the parish which he had served faithfully for 37 years. Mr. Hyett claimed in his will to have procured the school in the churchyard and left a sum for its endownment, though John Bradley, a Croston priest had obtained permission to open a school as early as 1372.

James Pilkington died after twenty-one years. His successor, Charles Layfield B.D. figured in an unusual dispute with local farmers who refused to pay tithes on potatoes because "tithes were on corn." He took the case to the high court in 1685 and won. The potatoes must have been the first grown in Lancashire because the seed was obtained when a ship carrying it from Ireland was wrecked near Hesketh Bank!

There were a number of other changes before James Pilkington's son, William Pilkington Ll.D. became rector in 1703, and purchased the living. He held the office for fifty years and brasses in the church commemorate not only him but his wife, Alice, of whom it is said "As she always spoke her mind, her aversion was very much against flattery, compliments and hypocrisy. Her visits to the rich were rare, but frequent to the poor."

24

A 'Granny Dear' Band in Croston Coffee Day, 1902.

In a corner of the churchyard a school founded by a Puritan.

25

'KING CROSTON'

Streynsham Master D.D., who had married Margaret, daughter and heir of Dr. Pilkington, became the next rector and the Master family held the living close on 140 years and provided five rectors. Streynshaw Master (great nephew of the first one) was known as 'King Croston' and drove a coach and four. Croston had one of the first savings banks in 1818, thanks to his foresight. Rector for 66 years, he died in 1864 at the age of 97.

Although the name changed in 1894, the Rev. A. G. Rawstorne who became suffragan Bishop of Whalley and Archdeacon of Blackburn, was his great grandson. The Rev. R. A. Rawstorne who succeeded in 1932 was the son of Bishop Rawstorne.

Whether or not battles were fought near Croston is Saxon times, life in the village through the centuries seems to have been peaceful enough. Even the Civil War, which touched it little, although a record of 1644 explains that many were unregistered by reason of Prince Rupert coming into Lancashire and this book was hid in fear of the enemies taking it. This book was the register. The registers of marriages and burials began in 1538, and for baptisms in 1543 but the earliest volume preserved in the church begins in 1728.

If the castle continued in Norman times there seems to have been no need to give it a more permanent form in stone.

Roger de Montbegon, Lord of Hornby, who held it for the king perhaps felt that he had castles enough. As happened in so many places the manor house replaced the castle. A farm close to the river still bears the name and to get to it one crosses the wonderful Town Bridge.

MANOR DIVIDED

The manor of Croston was early divided because in 1300 John de la Mare was succeeded by two daughters. Isobel married Sir John le Fleming of Wath and this half of the manor continued in the family until 1470, when it was split again through failure of the male heir. One daughter married Richard Dalton, Lord of Bispham and the other Thomas Hesketh and though this latter marriage was annulled and the heiress married one Thurston Hall, Thomas kept the Lancashire part of her inheritance.

As a result, in 1558, Sir Thomas Hesketh, who inherited it, was able to reunite the half manor by purchase.

The other daughter of John de la Mare married William de Lea, and this half of the manor descended to the Ashtons when Alice de Lea married Thomas Ashton.

The arms of Ashton (a chevron between three garlands), and Lea (three bars), of Dalton (a lion rampant between eight crosses crosslet) and Fleming (six bars and three lozenges in chief) are carved in stone, over the ancient north door of the church.

Other local families including the Hesketh's and the Banastres are included in the church heraldry.

26

William Farrington of Worden obtained the faculty for holding three pews in the church by right of his estate at Littlewood, in 1585—a fact which is made clear on the carving on the woodwork.

CATHOLIC FAMILY

The Ashtons and their successors the de Traffords were the chief resident family for three hundred years. Thomas and Richard Ashton were avowed Roman Catholics, and Richard who succeeded his brother was charged with recusancy and delinquency in spite of his protest that he had "lived peacably at home during these troubles." The estates were sequestered.

It was Richard Ashton's daughter and heir who married Sir John Trafford of Trafford and the estate went to that family.

Their son John registered as a Papist in 1717. In 1874 John Randolphus de Trafford bought the other half of the manor so that one more Croston had one lord. He died in 1879 and was succeeded by Sigismund Cathcart de Trafford whom many remember. During his time a court leet was held regularly at Croston Hall.

He was succeeded by Mr. Jeffrey de Trafford the last lord of the manor of that name.

Most of the history of Croston, however, seems to centre not round the big landowners but the church. It was so to speak a feudal benefice held in fee. Some people hold that the old Coffee Day Festival originated in fact from the Foeffing Day when tenancies were renewed.

Approaching Church Street from the east.

27

In the 18th and 19th centuries of course the church provided the local government. In 1715 the wardens were allowed 25s. a year expenses and sidesmen 5s. with a possibility of a 1s. fine for being absent from church. This restriction seems to have been imposed because when bargaining to get the lowest price they spent what they saved in ale.

The price of a bell wheel was bargained at 1s. 6d., but the same amount was spent in refreshments. Like their Saxon ancestors, the parishioners of Croston liked their ale!

Even today Croston has half-a-dozen inns, and they are picturesque ones too. When courts were held at Croston before the war we used to adjourne to the Grapes almost next door. This was a friendly court, where the press sat at the same table as solicitors. But then Croston is a friendly, hospitable place.

"BEGGAR" BENEFACTOR

This seems to have gone on through the generations for the charities are quite numerous. The best known is that of Peter Lathom of Bispham, who although a descendant of the Lathoms of Parbold, is said to have lived by begging in the townships which now benefit under his will made in 1700.

He directed that the income should be given to the poor in cloth, corn, if it should be dear, and such charitable acts, but that no public officer or overseer of the poor should be employed in this distribution. The poor prisoners of Lancaster Castle were also remembered.

The variety of ways of distributing this charity was increased in 1879 by the Charity Commissioners.

The village is also well provided with alms houses. The oldest has a tablet over the door announcing that it was erected by Henry and Isabel Croston in 1692. The jubilee almshouses near to Fishery Bridge were founded in 1809 to commemorate the 50th year of the reign of George the Third, a legacy of £200 by Mrs. Elizabeth Master starting the fund.

Further rooms were added in 1870 by Thomas Norris. The endowment provides for maintenance of the buildings and also coal.

Squire Geoffrey de Trafford was present in September, 1953, when a new cross was placed on the old base in Church Street. The cross was cut from an old millstone given by Mr. T. Dalton, third generation of his family at the smithy close by. It was a ceremony which somehow united all kinds of interest and all kinds of times, and really seemed to bridge the centuries of this charming village.

CHAPTER FOUR

HIGHWAY TO LATHOM

The Wardens of Croston Parish Church may have had good reason when they hid the register in 1644 'by reason of Price Rupert's coming to Lancashire.'

Quite apart from the fact that every large force took what it wanted in the name of the King or Parliament, Prince Rupert, the king's nephew, had a reputation for ruthlessness. Only in May that year he had refused to give quarter to the vanquished at Bolton, and put 1,200 to the sword after winning the town. For this, Lord Derby was to pay later with his head.

Prince Rupert, was related to Lord Derby's wife, the Countess de Tremoulle, heroine of the seige of Lathom House, then the seat of Lord Derby.

Lathom was too close to Croston for comfort. If you cross the Yarrow at the old water mill and follow Syd Brook (it means South Brook) to Mawdesley, it is but a hop, skip and a jump through the village to Bispham Green, which is on the edge of Hosker Moss. Through Hosker Moss runs the highway to Lathom.

No doubt much traffic took this road in those days. Colonel William Farington of Worden and his son Capt. Farington and possibly Robert Charnock of Astley and others who were officers in the seige of Lathom House rode along here.

Mawdesley itself is a sort of village where one expects to find a squire. At the turn of the century it had two, Sir George Fermor Hesketh of Rufford, and Mr. Sigismund Cathcart de Trafford of Croston. Manor courts were held annually at the Black Bull, better known locally as 'Ell 'Ob because of its giant poker.

Although there was no residential lord and Mawdesley descended pretty much with Croston, there is a charming old hall built on an outcrop of red sandstone in Hall Lane. From the roadway a stone staircase leads to the garden of what has every appearance of being an old manor house.

The centre portion of the house is 17th century, for cut in the large stone over what was once an open fireplace, are the initials of William Mawdesley and the date 1625. A fresco in plaster over this stone carries the Mawdesley arms, and the date 1655, which is probably when alterations or additions were made by Robert Mawdesley whose initials also appear in the plaster.

Robert Mawdesley died in 1659 and left to his son Alexannder, two signet rings 'wishing he would make them both into one signet and thereto set his coat of arms and leave the same to the heir's male.'

This part of Mawdesley is known as the City. The stone building beyond the white cottage is City Farm. Further along still, where the road turns sharply to the left, is "Towngate." At the other end of the village is High Street.

Lane End House in Smithy Lane, the home of the Finches. One window is said to mask a priest's hiding place.

The coat of arms was probably a sign of increasing prosperity of the family although the name appears in land dealings as far back as the 14th century.

The arms are unusual in that on a black shield is a silver chevron between three silver pickaxes and on the chevron, are three black rings or annulets.

The proof of the increasing prominence of the family was that Alexander's son and heir, another Robert became sheriff of Lancashire in 1720. His son Thomas left the estate to the Rev. Thomas Mawdesley of Astley and after that it was acquired by Alexander Kershaw of Mawdesley, and in 1870 by the Bretherton family of Eccleston.

On the other side of Towngate, land was held by a family called Nelson who registered a pedigree in 1613.

Henry Nelson for his part in the Civil War had his lands sequestered but he got them back again on paying a heavy fine. A son Michael Nelson, also appears to have been involved in the war for about this time he was trying to sell land to get himself out of prison.

A local yeoman who got into trouble for a different cause was William Clifton. He was executed in 1562 as one of those responsible for the murder of William Huyton of Blackrod.

RELIGIOUS PERSECUTION

Most of Cromwell's sequestrations in the district were not on account of the civil war, but religion. There is a pitiful pleading by Thomas Rutter's widow, Elizabeth, who petitioned that she was 'ever a good Protestant' and her five children were 'all likely to starve unless the sequestrations were taken off.'

Thomas Finch, one of Mawdesley's many yeomen, had two thirds of his estate sequestered for recusancy only.

Gillow's bibliographical dictionary records that the Finches of Mawdesley suffered from heavy fines for recusancy. Henry Finch, his son Thomas, and grandson Henry appeared in the rolls during the reigns of Charles I and Charles II.

Lane Ends House in Smithy Lane, their home, is still standing. It has always been said that it has more windows outside than in because one covers the priests hiding place.

I have often heard of chapels in the rooftops used during the persecution, and in this beautiful old building which goes back to the 16th century, I have at last seen one! It has recently been restored and is used for worship.

Preserved in a glass case under the altar is the skull of the monk, Brother William Haydock, who was hung, drawn and quartered at Whalley in 1537, following the Pilgrimage of Grace. This, along with other relics, portraits of the Haydock family (one said to be William) and a hatchment of the Haydock arms, came from Cottam Hall.

The chapel in the roof at Lane End House is still used for the Mass.

Not a manor house, but looking very much like one, Mawdesley Hall goes back to the 17th century.

The Finches and the Haydocks were related by marriage and in 1714, the Rev. Cuthbert Haydock came to Mawdesley as Chaplain. He was the younger brother of Squire Haydock of Cottam who the following year paid the penalty along with Richard Chorley and others for taking part in the Jacobite rising.

FARMER DIED FOR FAITH

Apart from fines and sequestrations, the Finches had already had a member of the family who had died for the faith. Blessed John Finch was not a priest, but a farmer who had been brought up as a Protestant, but on reconciliation served as a contact man between the clergy and those in the faith who needed a priest. It was while carrying out such a mission that he was deceived by a renegade Catholic, who was a pursuivant spy. This led to capture, of John Finch and the priest he had produced one Father George Ostcliffe.

At the time only a proportion of religious persons were chosen for execution and that one of those should be John Finch is measure of his determination not to recant. It is recorded that he was a man of great physical strength and it took a posse to drag him by the heels to attend state service. He was also made to suffer in horrible privation, in a dungeon on a bridge of the river. He died, professing the faith on April 20th, 1584.

It is fitting that the Mass should still be said regularly in the chapel, which until the church of St. Peter and St. Paul was built in 1831, was the only place for worship the Catholics of Mawdesley could attend.

Mawdesley today is in process of renewal. Smart bungalows appear in the street where there are also cottages, white-washed, half-timbered or in stone and barns at the roadside proclaim farming is still king. Yet somehow, they don't look out of place. The new village is blending with the old in a charming fashion.

MAWDESLEY BASKETS

When I was a lad, Mawdesley's chief claim to fame was basket making. It is still the local industry, next to farming.

I chanced to see at work on this craft, Stanley Dalton in High Street. He was sitting on the ground in the open, making a potato hamper from rods which he had grown and cut himself. These are stacked and to make them pliable for use, boiled in a 12 foot boiler.

In 1871, Mawdesley had named Cobham, also a Bentham, a Harrison, a Walker, and a Walsh and Thomas Mawdesley.

Local street names suggest that Mawdesley was quite an occupational centre in days gone by. At least there is a Smithy Lane at one end of the village, and a Tannersmith's at the other. There is also a Tinckler's Lane, but this is probably called after one of the local yeomen, not a tradesman.

Bispham Hall may have been the home of the Nelsons, another Mawdesley family, who belong to the Fairhurst branch. The sundial at the front is an unusual feature of the building.

The school at Bispham. It began as a free grammar school and had a reputation for teaching classics.

Salt Pit Lane is an indication that saline springs in the district used to be pumped for brine to make salt. The deep shafts are still there at Salt Pit Farm. In front of the farmhouse, the oldest part of which goes back to 1692, is a well of fresh water, which they say never runs dry. Before water came out of the tap, people journeyed miles to this well during the droughts.

There is also a tradition that there was a monastery close by, which is not surprising in view of the strong Catholic community in the village.

Another lane, which an occupational tinge is Malt Kiln Lane, which runs through Bispham which has a green flanked by rosy bricked council houses on one side, and an olde worlde public house the Eagle and Child, on the other.

Further on there is also a fine old house known as Bispham Smithy. Turning left at Chorley Road, one has a fine view of Harrock Hill, and comes to the Farmers Arms and the grammar school.

The school was founded in 1692 by Richard Durning (whose initials appear in the stonework) as a free grammar school, and for a period had the reputation for teaching classics to girls as well as boys. Latin was taught as late as 1825. but the school later became an elementary school and was extended in 1939.

It is right on the boundary of Bispham and Wrightington and in consequence provides the polling station for two parliamentary divisions in general elections, Chorley and Westhoughton.

LINKS WITH CHORLEY

This township which has the name of a seaside resort has very old links with Chorley, and in 1332 it was known as Chorley with Bispham.

In 1338 it was referred to as the 'hamlet of the ville of Chorley.' This could be explained by the fact that like Chorley, it belonged to the Ferrers family.

From them the Daltons held it as early as the 14th century. Sir Robert de Dalton and his son Sir John, fought at Crecy in 1346. For all that, Sir John fell out of favour with the king because on Good Friday, 1347, assisted by Sir Robert de Holland, Sir Thomas de Arderne, and other friends, he abducted forcibly, Margaret de la Beche from her manor near Reading. This was right under the nose of the king's son Lionel, who was keeper of Reading and could not therefore be ignored.

Sir John and his companions under threat of arrest, fled to Lancashire, and so involved other members of the family who gave them refuge and the priors of Up Holland and Burscough.

Sir John was later pardoned for 'good service.' Presumably his performance at Crecy had stood him in good stead.

He married the lady he had abducted, but when he died in 1369 his heir was a six-year-old boy by a later wife. The manor eventually descended to a daughter and was sold to the Stanley's of Lathom. It then became part of the Derby state.

The estate, held by a younger son of John de Dalton descended to Robert Dalton and in 1558, he sold it to William Stopford. His hall was known as Bispham Hall, and is probably the one with the sun dial which overlooks the fertile plain of Hoscar.

But there is now no journey to Lathom House. After the second seighe, Cromwell's men flattened it so that even the site is disputed.

Stanley Dalton sits down on the ground to make a hamper in the traditional fashion. The basket industry, which made Mawdesley famous, began because rods grown in Mawdesley were stronger and more pliable than those grown anywhere else.

CHAPTER FIVE

THE ROBIN HOOD COUNTRY

Lancashire is noted for the number of its small farms. This is due to the sale of the property of the religious houses by the Crown, when parcels of land were acquired by many who had previously been occupiers only, also partly due to the independent spirit of those who tilled the soil. They developed a middle class between the gentry and the labourer. They were the yeomen, countrymen, or men of the district.

Nowhere is the countryside richer in yeomen than from the point where Syd Brook and Howe Brook meet to the hills of Harrock and Hunter's. It is significant perhaps that near the meeting of the two brooks there is a Robin Hood Inn and a Robin Hood Well, and at the other side of the two hills, the whole district is known as Robin Hood. Robin Hood was the equivalent of a patron saint for the yeomen.

The Heskin part of this country is generally confused with Eccleston at the one end and Wrightington at the other, but for those who live there, the division is plain enough. It has its own village, Heskin Green, where there is also a grammar school. It also used to have two coal mines. One down the valley of Syd Brook which is the boundary, was known as Basket Pit because coal was brought up in baskets.

The grammar school was founded in 1597 by Sir James Pemberton, who became Lord Mayor of London, and was not ashamed to claim Heskin as his birthplace.

Another distinguished son of Heskin was Thomas Heskin, a Dominican and a scholar, who was deprived of his living by Queen Elizabeth I and had to flee abroad.

Carrying out a different role was Sir William Fleetwood, a noted lawyer who was M.P. for Lancaster from 1559 to 1567. He was also said to have been born in Heskin. He seems to have had a reputation for severity in executing the laws against vagrants and Catholics. He was an authority on the Duchy of Lancaster, on which he wrote a short history.

NO SUCH PLACE

For along time, Heskin had no manor. Robert de Heskin claimed part of the lordship in 1323, but he was turned down on the grounds that the place was part of Eccleston. At any rate he tried, which showed independence of spirit by a yeoman, even in those early days.

Heskin Green – the town of the township.

Barmskin Hall – the name relates to brewing beer – like maltkiln.

Heskin has two interesting hamlets — Barmskin Green and Bannister Green, both on Howe Brook, which rises in Harrock Hill and meanders through this lovely countryside of fertile fields where the corn grows high and where the cattle feed well in the luscious pasture. It gives name to an inn, the Brook House (formerly the Windmill). This is at Barmskin, which is linked to Heskin Green by Town Lane.

Barmskin Hall is a stone built farmhouse with an inscription over the front door which has eroded so much that it cannot be read. This is most exasperating! All the same, it is a pretty place, particularly at hay time when the laburnum is out.

At Banister Green there is a Howe Brook House, part of which is half-timbered and evidently a great age. The stone built barn is also half-timbered on one side and looks older still. One has to be quick to get a glimpse of these buildings from the road, for it is a nicely wooded here and in summer the lane from Eccleston Green goes through a tunnel of leaves.

Further on, a neat white-painted cottage comes to view. It bears the name Anderton's School and some of the older residents remember it as a Dame's School. Apparently they had to pay ha'pennies to attend, until a legacy was left by a member of the Anderton family.

Perhaps it is the school which earned Halfpenny Lane across the way, its name. On the other hand one wonders if the lane to Barmskin Green was a turnpike and this lane was the means of taking a short cut to Tanners Lane and the Robin Hood. The alternative route is a long one, via Threaper's Green which could be another way of saying Three Posts Green, another suggestion of turnpikes. This, however, is sheer speculation for the old maps show the only turnpike at Wrightington Bar.

Halfpenny Lane seems to continue the private road past new Heskin Hall to form a link with old Heskin Hall.

WATCHING THE BOUNDS

In Heskin, a contradictory situation exists because the new hall is older than the old. The present old hall occupies the site of a much older one demolished 150 years ago. It is right on the boundary with Mawdesley and was possibly built there to keep an eye on the bounds — a not unusual practice with manor houses.

Blackburn House across the way, is in Mawdesley and was probably built for a similar purpose — to keep an eye on Heskin. It may be the same age as the original Heskin Hall and it certainly contains some interesting wattle and daub inner walls.

It was probably occupied by one of the Nelsons, the Mawdesleys, the Stopfords or other yeomen who held land in Mawdesley.

Heskin did not become a manor until it was acquired by Sir Richard Molyneux. As in the case of Mawdesley, the absence of a resident lord resulted in local families becoming important. Apart from the bid for the local lordship, the surname Heskin is mentioned as early as 1301, when

Harrock — the crop grow right up the top where stands the old windmill tower.

Like Harrock, Hunter's Hill is long and low. The School Farm on the left would be part of the endowment of Bispham School nearby.

Richard de Heskin was a juror, which proved he was a yeoman, for one specialised definition of that term was to possess free land worth 40/- annually — a qualification for jury service.

Other families holding land in Heskin included de Hoghton, Rutter, Banastre and Lancaster.

One of the biggest landowners was Thurston Mawdesley of neighbouring Mawdesley. His possessions included new Heskin Hall which he acquired from Sir Richard Molyneux, in the reign of Charles I. The building is of an attractive weathered brick and is generally ascribed to the 16th century. The initials of Alexander Mawdesley were found on part of the building with the date 1670, but this most likely related to alterations or additions.

The Mawdesley estate was acquired from 1739-1744 by Alexander Kershaw, who seems to have settled in Heskin.

Though he never married, he had a number of children, and in his will of 1786 three of these Edmund Newman, John Cooper and James Kershaw were named as his heirs. In fact, after Alexander's death in 1788, first Edmund Newman and then John Cooper succeeded in turn. As neither had left a lawful issue as required by the will, the estate was claimed by heirs of Alexander's sister Mary.

RUNAWAY BRIDE

On her wedding day Mary is said to have run off with a man who was taking her to church on the pillion of his horse. His name was Ralph Stott and the couple lived together for over 50 years. Although there was no evidence that they were married, a jury in 1833 decided that they were, as they had always been regarded as married. In consequence, Mary's descendants won the case.

Not mentioned amongst the early landowners in Heskin or Wrightington, are the Andertons. This is curious because Anderton Mill which is not far from Threaper Green and is both in Mawdesley and Wrightington must have been important. The mill has disappeared but there is a circular stone base near the mill cottage which remains. The date over the door of the cottage is 1799 but there may have been an older building on the site.

It would appear that the Anderton's in this district stemmed from the Andertons of Euxton. This family bought and sold land in various parts of the county and one of them actually sold Worden to the Faringtons.

The fact that they had the mill suggests that they may also have had a share of the manor, for the right to mill corn was usually invested in the lord of the manor.

It is recorded that in 1508, Nicholas Rigbye of Harrock Hall made a settlement on his son and heir also Nicholas, who was to marry Margaret daughter of Hugh Anderton of Euxton. Like the Anderton's the Rigbye's were staunch Catholics, and it was one of Nicholas's younger sons who became Blessed John Rigbye, who was hung drawn and quartered at St. Thomas Waterings in London in 1600. As he was dragged through the

41

Heskin Hall – a stately place once owned by Sir Richard Molyneux.

Anderton's Mill before the mill tower was demolished.

streets, he called to the crowds "I am a poor gentleman of the house of Harrock of Lancashire. My judgement and condemnation to this death is that I said I was reconciled to the Catholic Church and refused to go to the (State) Church."

His eldest brother, Nicholas, who succeeded to Harrock was a convicted recusant in 1628. After that however, there seems to have been a change in the family for the next heir, also Nicholas, fought on the side of Parliament in the Civil War, Nicholas was a captain and county commissioner. He was also presumably, Protestant.

Colonel Alexander Rigbye who was MP for Wigan, also a noted officer for Parliament in the Civil War, belonged to the same family. The Rigbye's who somehow contrived to maintain a succession of Nicholases at Harrock for several generations, were landholders here from the 13th century.

Until the confiscation of religious houses they held the estate of the Knights Hospitallers. This would account for the tradition that there was a monastery in the neighbourhood.

WINDMILL LAND

Anderton's windmill must have been in close proximity to the one at Barmskin and the one which still remains, partly ruined, at Harrock Hill. Possibly it is a tribute to the fertile soil that so much corn was available for milling. At any rate the three mills were linked by road and from Anderton's Mill one can run straight up Harrock along Sanderson's Lane and from Barmskin along Coopers Lane. These must be fairly old roads because where they join is the base of a wayside cross.

The best way to see this lovely countryside is on foot and fortunately there are plenty of foot paths signposted.

By road the nicest run is to follow Bentley-Lane to Bispham Lane (just opposite Bispham School) and then climb up Banister Brow. On the left is a wonderful view of Harrock Hill with the old windmill standing on top. Screened by the trees there is also a glimpse of Harrock Hall, once the home of the Rigbye's.

Hunter's Hill is still as popular for picnicking as it was when I first went there in a wagonette from school! The road goes over the top and the view of the countryside, with the crops growing right up the hills calls to mind Psalm 65—"The little hills rejoice on every side. The pastures are clothed with flocks; the valleys also are covered over with corn; they shout for joy; they also sing."

From the top of Hunters Hill on one can continue along High Moor past the Rigbye Arms and the High Moor Club (built in 1462), to Robin Hood Lane, which leads to Dangerous Corner if you turn right, and Fish Ponds if you turn left.

But do not miss Hill Dale, the village belonging to Hunters Hill. It is in Chorley Road, past the Bispham School. It's worth a visit even if only to turn down Robin's Lane to Bispham!

43

Once an old dame's school – Anderton's School.

CHAPTER SIX

PRESBYTERS AND PRIESTS

Hill Dale is so close to Parbold that most people think it is part of it. It is however, in the township of Wrightington. So is Fairhurst Hall, once the seat of the Nelson family, who held land in the district until the 18th century, and who in the early days were among the tenants of the Hospitallers.

The Nelsons were strongly Catholic and at one time their home was the mission centre for the county round about. Now appropriately enough the Roman Catholic Church of Our Lady and All Saints in Parbold, built in 1884, is close by. It is served by Benedictines, an order in which some members of the Nelson family became monks.

In the Civil War, Maxie Nelson, a captain on foot in the King's Army is supposed to have lost his life at Marston Moor. Parliament ordered the sequestration of the estate but Maxie's son and heir, Thomas compounded on payment of £699–a stiffish sum in those days.

The present Fairhurst Hall is a compact Georgian building admirably sited at the foot of a grassy slope. The older part which contained the upstairs chapel has been demolished however.

If we follow the River Douglas, which flows close by, we shall come to a spot at the foot of Parbold where the ancient chapel of St. Mary used to stand. The building was demolished in 1875 when the new church was built on Parbold Hill, but the spot is marked by a cross carved from the old threshhold stone, and erected in 1906.

This states that the old stood here for four full centures–'loved by those who worshiped God from the country round about.'

The stone also records that the chapel existed in 1526 and was rebuilt in 1621. The Holy Table, the pulpit desk and font were removed to the new church.

A chapel is mentioned in records as far back as the 13th century, and may have belonged to the hospitallers. Across the way, is Prior's Wood a reminder that they were considerable land-owners here-abouts.

Following the Reformation, the old chapel would be a Protestant island in a sea of the old faith. In consequence it may not have been used at all.

This was changed as time wore on and the Rectors of Eccleston had the gift of the living.

Fairhurst Hall – a compact Georgian mansion in an attractive setting.

PAPISTS

The old faith persisted however, for as late as 1804 the incumbent reported to the Bishop that there were 67 Papists in his chapelry, and they assembled to worship at Wrightington Hall, Parbold Hall and Fairhurst Hall.

At Parbold Hall, the priest was called Marsh, which by coincidence is the name of the present priest at St. Joseph's, Wrightington, Father Vincent Marsh!

St. Joseph's which is reached by climbing over Parbold Hill, was built in 1892. It is across the way from Wrightington Hall, now a hospital.

Geoffrey de Wrightington was Lord of the Manor as early as 1282 and the family also had the manor of Welsh Whittle and lands in Coppull. As will be gathered, they too were members of the Catholic Church. Sir Edward Wrightington of Grays Inn was a Royalist and was removed from the list of J.P.'s in 1642. There is a memorial to him at Standish Church, erected by his nephew and heir, Hugh Dicconson.

The Wrightington estate descended to the Dicconson's, whose rather complicated coat of arms includes the hind's head, a favourite sign at inns in these parts. There is one at Dangerous Corner, one at Mossy Lea and one at Welch Whittle.

The Dicconsons carried on the Catholic tradition and William Dicconson described as a zealous Jacobite, had his land confiscated. He died in exile at St. Germain in 1743.

Roger, a younger brother was outlawed after the 1715 rising. Sir Edward Dicconson, professor at Douai and afterwards Bishop of Malla and Vicar Apostolic of the northern province, resided at Finch Mill, Shevington and is buried at Standish church, where there is a memorial to him.

In a part of the country so strongly papist, it is perhaps not surprising that on one side of Moss Lane, which runs past St. Joseph's Church from the Fishponds, is a wood called Low Courage, because it is said, of the feeling of Cromwell's men when they approached such dangerous country.

Be that as it may they had staunch Presbyterian country at their backs. South Tunley Hall was the home of the Wilsons and Thomas was a member of the Presbyterian Classis in 1646.

His initials and those of his wife and the date 1622 appear over the porch of the Hall. A downspout also carries the family crest of the demi-wolf.

The approach up steps to the garden is singularly charming; over one of the archways the initials T.W. – M.W. are repeated again and the date 1671.

Near the River Douglas here, was Douglas Chapel.

47

This area must also have had its Quakers, for a farm now known as Charity Farm, one of a number associated with Peter Lathom's charity appears on old maps as Quaker Haydock's! This is off Smithy Brow just before you reach the Heskin border and the Brook House Hotel.

Going southwards, the lane is known as Toogood Lane, and leads right through to Tunley Lane.

It is an interesting old building known as Toogood Hall. It would be rash to try and fathom the origin of this name unless the Catholics were skitting the Puritans! The hall however has the initials W.H. and the date 1708 carved on the stone.

Old maps show that this was known as Heskin House. The Heskins held land in those parts and Thurston Heskin described as "of Wrightington" died in 1591.

PASTOR NOT PRIEST

South Tunley is reached from Toogood Lane by simply turning down Old Wash Lane, which leads to Tunley Lane and Mossy Lea Road. Mind you the best view of the hall is travelling from the main road.

Even Protestant owners of old buildings, like to think there is a priests hiding place somewhere about. If there is one at South Tunley Hall, it is for fleeing Presbyterian pastors, not Papist priests! Adam Martindale is said to have sheltered here, also Jonathan Schofield. Schofield was curate at the little chapel at Douglas in 1662 when on Black Bartholomew's Day, he and nearly 2,000 others refused to conform to the Act of Uniformity. He died in 1667, but must have left followers, for in 1691 was built at Mossy Lea not far away, Tunley Presbyterian Chapel, the oldest of its kind in England.

At any rate in 1691, only two years after the Toleration Act which gave freedom of worship to non-conformists, the Presbyterian Chapel was built at Tunley. The land was given by Mr. Wilson of South Tunley Hall. The original building had a capacity of 120, the school was added in 1881 and other additions were made in the 1950's.

A curious feature of the site of the church is that it practically adjoins Chisnall Hall. In fact Chisnall Hall Lane which used to join Mossy Lea to Coppull runs past the church.

The Chisnalls were anything but Presbyterian.

They had held land in the district from the 13th century and one of their number, Colonel Edward Chisnall was a noted officer on the King's side in the Civil War. He distinguished himself at the first seige of Lathom House and at Marston Moor. In the first stage of the war he was captured at Wigan and in the second one, at Appleby. His estate was sequestered on the grounds that "being newly called to the bar at Gray's Inn he had adhered to and sustained the force raised against Parliament."

After he had compounded he wrote "a Catholicke History in Defence of the Reformed Church of England."

It had a controversial theme which ignored altogether the fact that Parliament had made the English Church Presbyterian!

His son, Sir Edward Chisnall who succeeded him, may have had different views. At any rate, he was versatile. He was then MP for Wigan from 1688-9 as a Whig, and for Preston in 1690 as a Tory!

What makes this particularly interesting is that an old document produced some years ago quoted the Parliamentary Inquisitors of 1650 as recommending the building of a church in Coppull "in the same place where the old hall of Chisnall situate in Coppull formerly stood," and, "that a road be allowed by Edward Chisnall, owner of the inheritance."

Old Chisnall Hall itself has disappeared, although there are still signs of the moat.

The new Chisnall Hall is probably an 18th century building and set into one wall is a stone now somewhat eroded which probably carried the family arms — three crosslets fitchy in Bordure.

Toogood Hall — formerly known as Heskin House, once the home of one of the oldest families in the district.

Slag Heaps of Chisnall Hall Colliery, now closed, form a background to the hall itself.

South Tunley Hall – a Presbyterian stronghold in Catholic country.

Tunley Chapel – the oldest of its kind in England.

CHAPTER SEVEN

CHAPEL TROUBLE AT COPPULL

Tunley Brook which goes under the Wrightington Road (B.5250) at Rigbye Bridge changes its name to Stars Brook in Coppull where it is crossed by the Preston-Wigan Road (A.49) near the Seven Stars Hotel. The bridge there is known as 'Pongy Bridge' because it is said to be haunted. The brook then takes the name of Hic Bibi from a spring which is now piped into the brook.

The story goes that Cromwell, pursuing the remnants of the Duke of Hamilton's force towards Wigan paused at the well for a drink and finding it refreshing put up the inscription 'Hic Bibi', which means "Here I drank."

Whether "That Man" would have had time for such frivolities and whether he would have expressed himself in Latin if he had, is open to grave doubt. Much more likely is the theory favoured by the late Canon T. C. Porteus in "History of Standish."

This is that the well, being close to monastic land, the Latin name may have been a scholarly way of indicating that the water was fit to drink!

The well was sufficiently important to supply water to a number of buildings. One of these was Bogburn Hall, which it gets its name from the locality. The "bog" stands for Coppull Moor and the "burn" for the brook.

Previously the hall was Perburn which was also the name of the brook.

The hall which still stands, carries two stones, one on the porch and one on the gable dated 1663. The initials are those of the Haydocks and the one over the porch shows the sparrow hawks which appear in the arms of the family.

QUAKER SONS

The estate descended to the Haydocks from the Perburns in the sixteenth century. Roger Haydock who succeeded at the age of seven in 1622, probably rebuilt the hall as the initials over the porch could stand for those of himself and his wife, Alice.

Three of the sons of this marriage, John the eldest, and Roger and Robert became Quakers, but the fourth one, William, was inducted Rector of Standish in 1678.

The younger Roger, like his brother, John, spent much time in prison for his Quaker beliefs but he was released at this time probably to attend William's induction.

There does seem to have been some toleration shown in those days for Roger was allowed out of prison quite regularly so that he could preach and teach.

His son emigrated to New Jersey and in both Standish Church and Coppull St. John's are memorial tablets to the family placed there in the twenties by descendants in America.

When England was in turmoil chiefly because of Jacobite plots, Quakers and Catholics alike were suspect. John Haydock's house was searched for arms in 1683 and 1691. On the latter occasion he was suspected of having supplied weapons to William Standish, of Standish Hall, who took a leading part in the rebellion.

Having regard for the Quaker tradition of pacific resistance, the searches seemed rather peculiar even for those times. John in fact died in Lancaster Gaol in 1719 and was buried at the Quaker burial ground at Langtree for which the family obtained the land. Before they had the meeting place at Langtree, the Quakers met in the houses of their members, one of which would certainly be Bogburn Hall.

Coppull Parish Church. The old chapel on the site gave Chapel Lane its name. In the background is the school.

PERSECUTED

Not so far away at Blainscough Hall was another family as noted in the Catholic Church as the Haydocks were amongst Quakers. Blainscough had been in the hands of the Worthingtons from the early fourteenth century and when Elizabeth came to the throne Peter Worthington evidently meant to keep it that way.

At any rate he conformed to Elizabeth's religious settlement. His son Thomas, however, graduated at Oxford in 1570 when the treatment of recusants was 'hotting up.' He went to Douai and returned with the English Mission eight years later which must have caused some consternation to his father.

The father's attitude, however, was not shared by other members of the family. His grandsons Thomas, Robert, Richard and John followed the old faith and were put in prison by Bishop Chadderton.

Thomas who escaped along with his brother John, was taken again in 1584 when he was in company with his Uncle Thomas when he was betrayed at Islington. Uncle Thomas was sent to the Tower and later banished. He became President at Douai but returned in 1616 to England where he died ten years later having entered the Society of Jesus which he had always admired.

Two of his nephews, John and Lawrence, also became Jesuits.

Nephew Thomas who was heir to Blainscough, married a niece of Cardinal Allen and deemed it prudent to reside abroad at Louvain, where he died. His heir William was on the King's side in the Civil War and the estate was sequestered when the family were in low water, with hardly sufficient to pay the heavy fines.

During these troublesome times Blainscough Hall like most manors would have its own chapel and the pre-Reformation chapel in Chapel Lane fell into disrepair. That is why the Commission recommended in 1650 that a new one be built. It is hard however, to believe, that Cromwell used it to stable his horses, as many say.

It was in 1654 that William Crook had a new chapel built on the site on Cow Moss. He was helped by the congregation who provided the labour.

This seems to have produced trouble when after the Restoration, the building was used as a parish church served by a curate from Standish. The curate came only once a month and money was put up for a resident priest. There was also a desire for the Presbyterian form of worship.

DEFIED BISHOP

One curate the Rev. Thomas Ingham appointed in 1705, caused a good deal of offence by reason of "immoral life" and the solemnisation of "clandestine marriages."

He was ordered to cease his ministry there but defied the bishop who then locked up the chapel. Mr. Crook the principal trustee was helped by other noted Presbyterians, including the principal trustee was helped of Rivington to break the door open.

It seems that the bishop was willing to licence the chapel for Presbyterian worship with the promise that Mr. Ingham must go, Mr. Crook, however, supported the curate who remained until 1715, when the chapel was closed.

Mr. Crook was killed in a duel with Captain Buckley of Buckley and his right in the building went to Lord Willougby who transferred it to Sir Henry Hoghton of Hoghton another leading Presbyterian, in 1733.

The Rev. George Hargreaves was nominated for the church by Sir Henry. During his time the chapel was rebuilt in 1758. The present church took its place in 1861. Five years later, a commiteee was formed to provide a public clock in Chapel Lane. This of course was added to the church.

Older than the present church building is the school across the road. Built in 1817, it was one of the first of its kind.

Coppull Moor School was built in 1874 to meet the needs of the mining village which later developed to the north of the township and resulted in the building of Methodist churches in Preston Road, and Spendmore Lane in 1903, the Anglican Church of St. John the Divine in 1912, and the Roman Catholic Church of St. Oswald's in 1928.

Bogburn Hall, once the home of a Quaker family and a meeting place of Quakers.

TOP OF THE HILL

The old village was obviously near the old chapel. The name Coppull means top of a hill and there is indeed a Coppull hill rising to 300 feet not far from Chapel Hillock on which the church stands.

The lanes around here particularly Coppull Moor Lane, give wonderful views of the Anglezarke hills and others. There is also plenty of countryside along Jolly Tar Lane (once known as Ragwhistle Lane) and Green Lane (indicating a village green).

It is along Green Lane that one comes to Coppull Old Hall. One part of this building is certainly constructed on very old handmade bricks. This probably occupies the site of an older manor house still.

Little is known however of the family who take their name from the place. There was a Thomas, Lord of Coppull in 1213. Richard de Coppull granted Perburn between 1230 and 1264 to Burscough Priory.

In 1461 the manor was sold to Sir Thomas Stanley and descended with Lathom. Edward Rigby of Burgh acquired it in 1600 from the Earl of Derby and it changed hands again in 1775 when it was acquired by a family named Livesey and in 1820 by John Hodson of Ellerbeck. Through the latter it descended to Viscount Cardwell.

Elmhurst, Preston Road, one of the pleasant old buildings that has survived the centuries in Coppull.

There is one part of Coppull which is seldom recognised as such. It is the bit round the Grey Horse in Wigan Lane (A.5106). Our old friend Hic Bibi Brook goes under the road at Coppull Mill Bridge and forms the boundary with Worthington.

It is said that Worthington and Coppull used to be one. That is not hard to believe for Coppull Mill Bridge Farm is actually in Worthington itself. Beneath the ivy on the porch of the farm house is a stone bearing the date 1694 and the initials F.I.L. The I is the old way of showing J. and the letters are supposed to stand for John Fisher and his wife.

Born at Mill Bridge was the Rev.John Fisher who became a Benedictine and served as Chaplain at Standish Hall.

Coppull Mill Bridge — what was once a mill stream runs under the Chorley - Wigan road and marks the boundary between Coppull and Worthington.

Coppull Old Hall, may be built on the site of the manor house of Coppull.

Coppull Mill Farm is over the border in Worthington.

CHAPTER EIGHT

AWA' TAE ABERDEEN

East of Coppull Mill Bridge, the stream which we have followed from Tunley becomes Buckow Brook. This is its last change of name for it joins the Douglas in two large reservoirs which help to supply Wigan with water.

Below the reservoir is the Worthington Works of the Bradford Dyers Association. There was a water mill here as far back as 1384. The water supply must have been exceptional for in 1791 Robert Crompton started to make paper – a process which is greedy for water. Half a century later, the business was described as a water paper mill. The owner in 1859 was the proprietor of the Morning Post.

Not until 1863 did the paper making cease and the mill change over to bleaching.

Across the road from the mill is a beautiful 17th century building of stone covered with maple which in August turns red.

This is known as the Mill House but has also served as a manor and an alcove lined with benches for seating six good men is still preserved as the place where the manor court met.

The Mill House descended with the manor of Standish and after the rebellion in 1715, when Ralph Standish who had taken part as a Jacobite was charged with treason, the leasehold was claimed by a family called Jolly whose name was frequently given to the mill.

Canon T. C. Porteus in his 'History of Standish' states that there is little doubt that the estate was part of the endowment of the chantry of the Holy Rood in Standish Church.

This end of Worthington is as easily confused with Standish as the other is with Coppull. The family who took their name from Worthington resided at a tall building less than half a mile away. It stands back from the road but is easily recognised as Worthington Hall by its half timbered front.

Over the porch is carved the date 1577 and the name Edwarde Worthington. The initials M.O. also appear in one corner. Edward was lord of the manor in 1578 and 1591. The family had held Worthington from early times prior to the 13th century and one of them gave land to the Abbey of Cockersand. They do not appear to have been involved in anything more exciting than disputes with the Standish family about cattle grazing.

The peaceful valley of the Douglas, crossed here by a footbridge or ford. This is on Adlington Common, quite near to the lodge of Adlington Hall. On the other side lies Blackrod's district known as 'Aberdeen'.

Worthington Hall with its half-timbered centre portion has survived the later manor house, Adlington Hall.

The Millhouse at Worthington once served as a manor. The stone walls are covered in maple which grows red in Autumn.

THREE DUNG FORKS

Possibly they were too preoccupied with cultivating the land, which is very fertile in these parts. Their coat of arms is in fact three dung forks, which may be a play on the word worthing which means manure. The estate continued in the family until 1690 when it was sold by another Edward Worthington.

There was a period in our history when the old landed families, particularly those impoverished by the Civil War, gave way to the new merchant classes. Nowhere was this more evident than on the road that runs from Chorley to Boar's Head. In the Nineteenth Century, this winding lane with its views of distant hills and undulating country must have echoed frequently to the sound of the horse and carriage.

At the Chorley end was Ellerbeck Hall on the Duxbury side of Eller Brook that marks the boundary with Worthington. Nothing of the hall remains but there are gate posts in Wigan Lane and the sweep of the land is a reminder that here was a park every bit as lovely as Duxbury.

The Ellerbeck estate was acquired in 1799 by John Hodson, who completed building the hall eight years later. He was Tory M.P. for Wigan from 1802 to 1820, being followed in that capacity by his son James Alexander Hodson.

There is a talent to John Hodson of Ellerbeck in Standish Church stating that he died on March 11th 1828. It was erected by Richard Cardwell his nephew who inherited the estate. Richard's brother Edward was a famous church historian and principal of St. Alban's Hall, Oxford.

Another distinguished member of the family who lived at Ellerbeck Hall was Viscount Edward Cardwell of Ellerbeck, a statesman and close friend of Robert Peel. Among the prodigious work he carried out was the reform of the army when he was Secretary of State for War under Gladstone from 1868 to 1874.

His trustees administered the estate after his death in 1886, and the hall became the residence of Admiral Fanshawe who is still remembered locally.

'CASABIANCA' POET

North Hall was another stately home along this road and that too has disappeared though the entrance is marked by a lodge. Among the distinguished residents there was Mrs. Felicia Hemans, the writer of "Casabianca" and other popular verse.

This was too, the home of Captain Charles Hutchinson R.N., with fifteen years war service behind him. He had been flag lieutenant to the Duke of Clarence, afterwards William IV. His wife was sister of the Rev. Garnor Baldwin, Vicar of Leyland.

Edward Edge Silvester, whose family established a charity for the poor if Chorley, and who paid himself for the building of the north aisel of Chorley Parish Church resided at North Hall until his death in 1840.

Near the North Hall lodge is a bungalow called Park View. It overlooks what was once the park of Adlington Hall the home of the Claytons. It was Thomas Clayton, merchant of Liverpool, who acquired the manors of Adlington and Worthington. The Claytons are said to have descent from the old landed family of their name, and their arms—a cross engrailed between four torteaux must have been displayed on the White Crow nearby, for it was known as the White Cross. There is also a Clayton Arms in Adlington.

The family certainly gained distinction in their sons. Grandson of Thomas, Richard Clayton, became Chief Justice of Common Pleas in Ireland. When he died in 1770, he was followed by his brother Edward Worthington, a major in the Ninth Dragoons for whom North Hall had been built.

His brother John succeeded three years later. He too had resided at North Hall for his son Richard Clayton, the most noted member of the family was born there. Richard is chiefly remembered as the first baronet, an honour conferred in 1774. He was Recorder for Wigan from 1815 to 1828 and Constable of Lancaster Castle. He was also a noted translator with many published works to his credit. He died in 1828 at Nantes where he was British Consul.

The title and estate went to his brother Robert, who lived to the age of 92. In that he had exceeded the span of the original Thomas Clayton by one year! Robert built new barns at Adlington and Worthington halls in 1835 and the datestones bear his initials and a hand for the hand of Ulster—the baronet's badge.

From a desire to keep the land in the family, the estate was put up for sale some years before his death and was acquired by General Robert Browne Clayton who had married Henrietta, daughter of the first baronet, and assumed her surname after his father-in-law's death.

According to Canon Porteus, he was no doubt the Major Browne in a painting of British officers being presented to Pope Pius VI in 1794. This used to hang in Adlington Hall and is now in South Kensington Museum.

The only son of this marriage died in 1886, and his son Lieutenant Robert Browne Clayton had been killed at Redan, Sebastopol. In consequence, Adlington Hall went to James Robert Browne Clayton Daubeny, heir to the general's daughter Eleanor.

SUPPORTED RICHARD III

The drive to the hall still links the Worthington and Adlington manors of the Clayton domain. Like Worthington, the Adlington estate goes far back in history. Walter de Adlington was Lord in 1202. The Adlingtons were of sufficient status to marry into other landed families such as the Asshawes of Hall o' th' Hill. Their arms were a cheveron between three antelopes heads.

Prior to the battle of Bosworth Field, John Adlington "sware that King Richard should wear ye Crown."

In 1644 another John Adlington was killed trying to save the crown of King Charles I at the seige of Chester. For this his father Hugh's estate was entreated by Parliament until he showed his title. It descended in 1664 to John's sister, wife of Samuel Robinson of Chester.

Another local landholder John Pilkington seems to have had second thoughts about the King's cause at the Civil War. Having borne arms for the King he went over to the other side. This did him no good however, for he had to compound to save his estate in 1651!

Another old family the Allansons still remembered by Allenson House near Rigshaw Bridge. Reginald Allanson was a notable landowner in the days of Elizabeth I.

The Claytons carried out their manorial duties in Adlington and in 1839 when Christ Church was built Sir Robert gave £500 towards the cost. He also gave the site for the National School.

An even earlier school was built in 1815 on Adlington Common. It still stands and the datestone over the door announces that "This school for pious and useful learning was built by voluntary subscription." The initials R.P.R. stand for Richard Perryn, Rector (of Standish).

It was not until 1842 that the district became a separate parish including Adlington, Anderton and Heath Charnock and Duxbury. In 1884, St. Paul's Church was built, Christ Church becoming a chapel at ease. Whereas in 1851 it had been remarked that Adlington had no dissenting chapel, the rest of the century altered that.

A stately home, now demolished. Ellerbeck Hall. Viscount Cardwell lived there, though in later days he made his home at the Nightingales in Rawlinson Lane.

64

Even in 1851 Adlington had a cotton spinning mill (Thomas Gerard), a calico printer (Pollitt Bentley), Huyton Bleachworks (Rule and Davies), a Mordant Manufacturer (connected with dyeing), and a charcoal blacking factory. In fact, industry had come early to Adlington, William Norris and Robert Anderton having weaving mills as early a 1824.

By 1851 the population had risen in fifty years from 470 to 1,090, but in the next fifty years rose even faster to 4,523.

Industrially, the township had many advantages. It was in easy reach of coal. It was also served by the canal and two railway stations, the old L. and Y. (Adlington) and the L. and N. W. (White Bear). Even in the last war this made the place look important from the air, and the enemy bombers gave it attention!

There is so much lovely country among the hills to the east, that one forgets Adlington Common. There is not much doubt that the old community was near here. They used the land before the enclosures of the eighteenth century and hedges sprung up in our countryside.

It is also near a river, and essential for communal life in early days. Curious it should be the Douglas. Yet it has been close at hand ever since I left Croston. In fact I have kept saying I must cross it. Now I have come to a spot where the valley it at its loveliest, and there is a foot bridge and a ford. And they tell me it leads to Aberdeen!

This school was built in 1815 by public subscription, when Adlington came under Standish Church, and is now a cottage.

CHAPTER NINE

BACK TO THE YARROW

Around a bend in the road one comes upon the view of a river far below, meandering through open country which seems to stretch as far as that hill everyone now knows to be Harrock. The cows, the inevitable black and white ones, graze in the green fields, but here and there are yellow patches that tell of ripe corn. Down in the valley is the little red church.

This is a view of Eccleston which makes people want to pause. Even as lads we used to stop and gaze across this valley with a pleasure we could not define.

At the bottom of the hill there was an old mill, the red sand stone walls of which matched the church. It was worked by a water wheel from the River Yarrow and we used to watch fascinated as the mill stream seemed to emerge frothy and triumphant, from the busy paddles.

Here too, was the genial miller wearing a sack for an apron and looking rather like a ghost because he was white all over. Here if you were lucky you would see the fine shire horses as they delivered the corn or carted away the flour.

This was a part of England which time could not change. Or so I thought! I was wrong. The mill has gone and in its place stands a neat red brick house.

Yet there is still something old world about this scene and as one crosses the river by the hump back bridge the lych gate comes suddenly to view and one plunges back into the past.

That is an illusion of course. Originally the approach was along a footpath which leads from the Farmers Arms to a gateway almost opposite the front door of the church. Even if I had not been told this I would have believed it because in England one seldom finds an old church like this without a pub close at hand.

The new approach is better, for quite apart the lych gate, it is planted with trees which form an avenue and screen the church so that one gets glimpses of it above the rows of gravestones which rise from the well kept turf.

Make no mistake about it. This is a graveyard of charm where death seems very far away and I am not surprised to find that people like to sit here among the village fore-fathers and enjoy the peacefulfulness of a place where if time does not stand still it has a very good try.

Even when the church clock strikes it has a peaceful note as if there is no need to worry about minutes and hours when centuries mean so little.

The River Yarrow flows past the red sandstone church.

Eccleston Green – Was this Grosgreen where the hundred court used to meet?

FRIENDLY

The church itself is a friendly building; perhaps the red sandstone gives it a rosy look. Or it may be the design, which although it has arches and pillars and could be severe, is slightly irregular. The porch is certainly out of true and one cannot help but feel that the niches at the top of the arch should contain the statue of the Blessed Virgin Mary from which the church takes its name.

There are seats inside the porch which somehow invite one to sit down and rest awhile before opening the heavy door.

According to the experts the tower and chancel belong to the fourteenth century, and the south aisle and porch were added in the fifteenth, although there was extensive restoration in the eighteenth century.

Whenever these changes were made, including the recent one of providing a new roof, everything blends together and with rare charm.

In the nave the atmosphere of friendliness continues and one is not surprised to find that the clock has another face for the benefit of the congregation. The only trouble is one has to turn around to look at it, which may not be too encouraging for a preacher who has been overlong in the pupit!

ECCLESIASTICAL

There has been a church in Eccleston since 1094, when it was granted in part along with Croston by Roger of Poitou to the Abbey of St. Martin of Sees in Normandy.

In face the very name Eccleston has been traced to the British Latin 'Ecclesia' which means church. This suggest that there was a church here before Norman times.

The first rector on record was John de Attilgre who was instituted somewhere around 1260. Not all who followed were priests. William de Lancaster had to be given leave to attend school before ordination. Ralph de Tunstall also had leave to study.

Both became Rectors of Croston, Tunsall in 1318 a year after a claim that Eccleston was a chapelry of Croston had been rejected.

The dispute can have done little good, for the living was vacant for a year. Then a priest Richard de Wamburge took over in 1319. He also became Rector of Croston from 1334 until his death 10 years later.

Following this were three changes in quick succession but in 1322 John Travers was appointed and held the living for 12 years. This may be misleading for although he was a priest he had at one time been Constable of Bordeaux.

A court official, he was in dept to the King and the money due to him was collected in payment two years after his death.

The old school now serves as a meeting room.

Known locally as the Manor House, Brick Hall was the home of the Dicconson's of Wrightington.

The Priory of Lancaster which also came under the Abbey of Sees made the presentations until 1337 when Henry de Haydock was presented by the King. The same thing happened at Croston of course. Church properties belonging to the religious houses abroad were treated as alien when the country was at war.

Henry de Haydock could have been a member of the local family of that name. At any rate he seems to have shown little shrift for the lords of the manor with whom he had a dispute about felling trees to repair the chancel. Perhaps they had the death watch beetle in those days, too!

There was a query about William de Hexham who followed de Haydock. He was the son of a priest and having been instituted in 1369, without the special dispensation required in such cases, was ordered to resign. He was, however, still in office in 1392.

BISHOP'S TOMB?

Perhaps the biggest mystery of all in this church is the tomb which has served as an altar on the south side of the chancel.

It bears no name, but a brass on the top displays a priest with a tonsured head, cassock, surplice and cope. This quite apart from its design puts it at pre-reformation period and some say it represents William Wall who was rector from 1493 to 1511. He was presented by the Earl of Derby, for in 1430 the King had granted the advowson to Sir Thomas Stanley.

William Wall and the Earl are credited with founding the chantry chapel, at the altar of the church.

Another authority suggests that the figure on the brass is a bishop but the only bishop to hold Eccleston was Richard Parr who became Bishop of Sodor and Man in 1635. He continued as Rector of Eccleston until his death in 1643.

His appointment to the Isle of Man would be through the Earl of Derby though the family had sold the advowson of Eccleston to Thomas Lathom of Parbold in 1596.

The long association of the Derby family with the Eccleston church is commemorated on the 15th century font, which has carved on the side panels not only the emblems of the passion but the Stanley badge, the eagle's claw, and the Legs of Man.

Richard Parr had previously been Rector of Ladbroke but had exchanged this for Eccleston with a previous rector Edward Brounker. Trafficking in rectories was not unusual in those times and some rectors scarcely every saw the place.

The house which gives its name to Red House Lane. Like Brick Hall, the red bricks are now covered with rough cast.

CONGREGATION'S CHOICE

This can hardly have pleased the parishioners and a rare expression of opinion on their part was the appointment of Edward Gee in 1643. Richard Lathom and the patron was a minor, so Lord Saye acting as guardian, allowed the people to choose. The man they picked was Edward Gee who had been a minister in Eccleston for some years and who had evidently endeared himself to the congregation.

This is rather remarkable for a neighbourhood was supposed to be strongly catholic. At any rate Gee turned out to be a Presbyterian and signed the Harmonious Consent in prayer and divine rights of civil magistrates.

He was buried on Oak Apple Day, May 29th, 1660, when Charles the II was proclaimed King.

This may have been prophetic for the new rector Thomas Mallory had been expelled by Parliament from Northenden. This living was restored and he continued to hold it with Eccleston. He must have favoured Eccleston however, for he was buried there in September 1671.

The next rector Robert Pickering had also been Rector of Croston where he had been deprived for a time, accused of a simony — a fairly common complaint in those days one might have thought!

In many ways the story of Eccleston church is that of the Anglican Church itself. From the 18th century the appointments followed the course which was usual in the reign of Queen Anne, where a living was acquired and a rector presented who was sometimes a member of the family.

Close on a 100 years ago the patron was William Bretherton who resided at Heskin Hall and the rector the Rev. Humphrey William Bretherton who has been succeeded by two other rectors of the same name.

The Brethertons have in fact been more than rectors at Eccleston. When I first came to the village they were in effect local squires as well, and the old rectory on top of the hill was a charming manor house.

Tablets in the church and gravestones carry names which are still current in Eccleston today.

A small brass on the north wall of the nave is to the memory of William Dickinson "sometime stewarde for the most honourable household of the high and mighty Princess Anne, Duchess of Somerset 1604."

In a church as old as this which originally served besides Eccleston and Heskin, Wrightington and Parbold and was attended by many noted local families, it is surprising to find so little heraldry. However, I did notice carved on the backs of chairs in the chancel the lion rampant guardant of Dalton, the three plates on a chef indented of Lathom, and the cross flory of Rigbye of Harrock.

In the churchyard it appears that some gravestones have been used twice. One bearing a cross and sword inscribed in the fashion of the early 15th century has superimposed the name of John Rigbye and the date 1766.

CENTRE OF JUSTICE

Eccleston, besides having ecclesiastical importance, was also a centre of justice. The court of the Leyland Hundred was held there in the early 13th century. As late as 1528 it was referred to as the Wapentake, the title for such meeting places. The actual site of the court is believed to be Eccleston Green.

A document dated 1323 refers to Crosgrene, in Eccleston and this name points to a place where a number of roads meet. There is also reference to Crossgates Green in 1390. According to Canon Porteus, hundred courts usually met at crossroads for convenience.

Amongst cases heard at Eccleston, was one in which Richard Standish who had tried to possess the Street at Heath Charnock while the family were out at church, summoned with trespass those who ejected him. The case failed.

The usual way to announce the courts was in the church.

The manor court produced some complaints at the time of Sir Henry Farington, who was accused of holding one without the knowledge of certain land owners. Sir Henry said that the warning had been given through the church on Sunday for the following Wednesday as required, but that Richard Tomlinson of Scarscow had warned a number of people not to appear, unless the Lord of Bradley was present, with the King's steward to take half the profits.

Sir Henry was also accused by Mary, the widow of Thomas Seymour of causing the court to be held in the name of the king only. This, Sir Henry insisted, he was entitled to do because as steward of the king's body, he had to summon tenants to take the oath in court that they would wear no badge except the Red Rose, and be ready to serve the king.

Though it was held by Ralph Gernett as part of his reward for being forester in the 13th century, Bradley was identified with the hundred court from early times. The Dacre family were local lords until it was forfeited after the battle of Towton Field in 1461, when Randle Dacre was killed, and his brother Humphrey who had also fought on the side of Lancaster, attainted with treason.

The king allowed most of the estate to go to Joan, grand-daughter of Sir Thomas Dacre and her husband Sir Richard Fiennes. After Humphrey Dacre had come to terms with the king and had much of his estate restored, Eccleston was one of the places Sir Richard was allowed to keep.

In 1506, the manor was sold to Edmund Dudley, the minister to Henry VII who was executed for treason. His lands were forfeited but later his son John was allowed some of them, including Bradley. John ultimately became the Duke of Northumberland.

Sir Thomas Seymour was mentioned in connection with Bradley in 1530 when the estate which was regarded as a manor, seems to have become divided.

It was in 1539 that the Seymour portion was acquired by Richard Molyneux.

The old mill at Eccleston.
(Sketched by Ernest Heyes)

Bradley Hall was one of the oldest of the Eccleston manors, but unfortunately it has disappeared years ago, though there are still traces of the moat.

The other half of the Eccleston manor belonged to the Waltons, and was sold by a daughter of William de Walton to Henry, Earl of Lancaster, in 1347.

Like other property of the Earls of Lancaster, it ultimately belonged to the king. When Sir Richard Molyneux acquired it in 1595 he became sole Lord of Eccleston.

After the Walton half of the manor of Eccleston had been sold the Waltons continued to hold land in the district, and this became known as the manor of Tingrave, which is supposed to be represented by Ingrave Farm. This is still surrounded completely by a moat although no evidence of the old building exists.

This estate went to the Radcliffe's and the Bartons of Smithhills. The manor of Tingrave is mentioned in a Barton deed of 1652.

This makes one wonder if one of the Bartons built Red House in Red House Lane, which has over the door carved in stone the initials 'B' (for the surname) and J.M. and the date 1673.

DICCONSON HOME

So far as Eccleston is concerned best known as the 'manor' is Brick Hall, which hardly answers the description today, because it has been pebble-dashed over.

Another thing which disguises it is that from the main road, one sees the back and not the front. This is because the road line was changed many years ago. It is however, a 17th century building of hand made brick on a stone base.

Although it was never a manor, it was the home of the Dicconson family, who were the most prominent residents locally. They held land not only in Eccleston, but in Euxton, Charnock Richard, Heskin and Wrightington.

Another local resident of note was Richard Shirebourne who was one of the lords of Leylandshire. Shirebourne House, now a farm, carries on the name.

Yet another old farm is Sarscow, which is supposed to be haunted by the Sarscow Lady. It used to be the home of the Tunstalls, but there is nothing in its history to give a reason for haunting, except a claim of dowery by Cicely, widow of Thomas Tunstall in 1374.

Although industry has come to Eccleston and the modern housing has developed apace, it remains unspoiled as one of the beauty spots on the banks of the Yarrow.

CHAPTER TEN
EUXTON'S FAIR ACRES

Not so very long ago, Euxton was a small village of the manorial type. At the top of one hill was a collection of cottages and the ancient church, and across the valley of Chapel Brook was the hall with its hundred acres or so of sweeping parkland.

Industry had come early to the place, but touched it lightly. At the foot of the steep hill with the pretty name, Daisy Hill, the River Yarrow had provided water power for centuries for the grinding of corn. The same power was used for making paper and spinning cotton. Thus the riverside hamlet of Pincock was born.

The mills did not obtrude, however. They were in the valley and out of sight. Even the late power driven mills in Dawber's Lane did not clash satanically with Euxton's fair acres. They were built of red stone and what remains of them today, hardly looks like a factory.

The first big change that came to Euxton was the building of the railways in the mid nineteenth century. The Preston-Bolton line and then the Preston-Wigan line came through and carved up the countryside. This gave Euxton two stations. One at Euxton Junction on the Preston-Bolton line, was approached by a bridge over the Preston-Wigan line near the Railway Tavern.

The other was in Euxton Lane (then called Know Lane) near the Bay Horse. The ramp from the road is still there.

It was some time later that Balshaw Lane station replaced this one, for the convenience of the Squire (some say), but more likely because industry was at that end of the village. Even today, Euxton boasts what Chorley has not–a station on the main London line!

In was in October 1837, when the new railway was under construction, that a culvert gave way and blocked the River Yarrow so that it dammed the valley as far as Yarrow Bridge, Duxbury. When the water broke through there was a tidal wave that swept away the corn mill and many cottages and left a wake of devastation as far as Croston, where the rectory and church were flooded.

After the railway, Euxton's biggest change was in 1936. This was when the news broke about the Royal Ordnance Factory. I remember the day well, Sydney Heaton, who owned the Bay Horse, gave me the tip. Sydney, who had been a professional footballer and in the days when I first knew him weighed 23st., was really a sort of unofficial squire of the village. A magistrate, rural district council chairman for many years, and a county councillor, his advice was sought on many things by the good people of Euxton.

Once a chapel of Leyland, Euxton Church, said to have been rebuilt by the Molyneux family in 1513, stands on top of a hill.

The Castle Houses always arouse interest in Euxton.
They are just off Dawber's Lane.

On the day that I called, nearly every farmer north of Euxton Lane had been to consult Sydney about official forms they had received about taking over their land. It seemed that such a vast area, could be for only one purpose and my first report predicted an aerodrome!

At any rate, the R.O.F. brought fame to the village, and many thousands, B.B.C. announcers included were soon stumbling over pronouncing the name, in which the 'u' is silent. Even 'Lord Haw Haw', who appeared to know so much about the factory, got it wrong when he broadcast from Germany that the R.O.F. had been bombed.

When one thinks of the thousands who came to the factory in war time each day, of the dwellers at the Highways Hostel and Washington Hall, it's really surprising how the pronunciation has survived. Not even the Americans, the Irish, the Scots or the Tynesiders could kill it.

It is a name that has puzzled a few. My old headmaster, whose treatise on the history of Leyland should be a standard work, suggested half humorously that a man called Heck had lived in the village, and that was the derivation of the local exclamation "Oh heck!"

In this he wasn't far wide of the mark, for that great authority on names, Professor Ekwall, who with a name like his own might have had a personal interest, suggests that the origin is in the Old English personal name of Aefic or Efic, which is phonetically very close to Eck.

Be that as it may, there is some satisfaction in the fact that the name has survived the centuries whatever else may have happened to the township.

COURTING COUNTRY!

The fields on which the R.O.F. was built had tender memories for some. Not only were they good agricultural land, but they were criss-crossed by footpaths that made pleasant walks. One I remember, starting at Rose Whittle in Leyland and led more or less diagonally to Euxton Lane somewhere near Whinney Lane. When I had to walk to Chorley, which was pretty often, that short cut was welcome I can tell you!

For me the most regrettable loss was of Old Worden at Leyland and Buckshaw at Euxton. Both these old halls are now within the perimeter of the factory, ad though they are protected by a Ministry of Works order, that's not much consolation when the public cannot get near.

In spite of the R.O.F. and other developments, the other side of Euxton Lane is largely unspoiled and from Washington Lane branch a number of other pretty lanes which make it good courting country! Perhaps it is appropriate that on this part of Euxton the United Stated Eighth Army Air Force should have have left their mark behind. The lane was called 'German' after a family who owned the land locally, for more than a century. But the U.S.A.A.F. objected to the word German at any price and had the name changed!

Armetriding Farm, Euxton, a fine old Elizabethan House, which has the date stone 1570 and the initials H.A.

Buckshaw Hall Euxton. This picture was taken in 1934.

BEAUTIFUL RUNSHAW

Perhaps the part of Euxton I know best is Runshaw, because until I grew up, I always thought it belonged to my own village of Leyland. It came as a shock to find that it didn't.

For me Runshaw had always spelled wide open spaces, for after that splendid avenue of trees near the hall, the country was all green fields, gently undulating so that from a bit of a hump like Nickson Hillock you could see for miles.

I never really liked the idea of building an aerodrome there (proposed in the early thirties) and gave a sigh of relief when it was decided to use Samlesbury instead. Now the motorway has gone through but still there's plenty left. May it long remain unspoiled.

When I was a lad, it was round these parts that people still talked of shooting and hunting. 'Owd Gerry Cornwell, the last gamekeeper at Euxton Hall, had retired to the Plough which is still known by his name. There he exhibited pheasants and such like proof of Euxton's past glory.

Game and Euxton go back a very long way. In 1301 the King, Edward I, granted Robert Holland of Euxton 'free warren' over his demense land. That would be the land attached to Euxton Hall.

The charter that gave Euxton free warren also provided for a market every week on a Tuesday, and a fair every year on the feast of St. Barnabas. This may be why the village of Euxton was known as the 'burgh'.

The de Holland lands went to the famous family in Molyneux of Sefton, through heiress Joan de Holland, who had married William Molyneux. The Charnocks of Astley were proud of their relationship with this family, as is born out by the display of the Molyneux arms at Astley Hall.

The manor of Euxton was held by Molyneux until 1729. After that the ownership was divided until it was united in the last century by William Ince Anderton.

ROYALIST MAJOR

The Andertons had been noted Papists and Royalists from early days. When Charles II marched from the north, in 1651, he released Hugh Anderton from Lancaster gaol, then spent the night at Euxton Hall. It is a tradition that the prince drank water from a local brook and finding it cool, said it was a 'Cul' (cool) 'Beck' (brook)–and the brook has been known by that name ever since, at Shaw Green, Euxton's prettiest hamlet. The brook, which starts at Shaw Hill, Whittle, is known as Chapel Brook near the church.

That Hugh Anderton had been imprisoned by the Roundheads was hardly surprising. In 1642, the year that he bought Euxton Hall, he was appointed Commissionary General to the Earl of Derby and given the rank of major. He had taken part in campaigns at Lancaster, Warrington and in Ireland. The Roundhead newspaper of the day described him as a "bloody papists", who "when Prince Rupert was at Bolton, boasted of being in blood up to his elbows in that cruel massacre."

79

Shaw Green—The two Shaw Green farms are straight ahead.

There are three Shaw Green farms in the Euxton hamlet of that name. This one known as Old Shaw Green has a datestone 1703 which may belong to an addition.

At the other side of Euxton Burgh, as the village was known, Major Edward Robinson, Parliamentarian, and supposed author of the 'Discourse of the warre in Lancashire.' *lived* .

In 1643, he and his troops were taken prisoner by Lord Molyneux and detained at Lathom House, so the major would hardly be on friendly terms with his neighbours!

He bought the estate at Euxton, the year after the defeat of Prince Charlie at Worcester, but his grandfather had been a free-holder in the parish in 1600.

Buckshaw Hall which is still one of the best examples of half-timbered buildings in the area, was built by Major Robinson about the time when his Royalist neighbour, Hugh Anderton, suffering again for the defeat of a royal master, had his entire estate sequestrated.

JACOBITES TOO!

In spite of the sequestration Hugh was 'not without', as they say, and on his death was succeeded by his son William who maintained the royalist cause by supporting the Jacobites. In 1689 he was imprisoned at Manchester because of his part in the Revolution which aimed to keep William of Orange off the throne.

The Royalists tradition brought further trouble to the family when William's son Hugh was outlawed following the 1715 Rebellion. The estate was forfeited and bought by William Brooke of London, youngest son of Richard Brooke of Astley, but this may have been an undercover deal to secure it for the Andertons, until Hugh, whose interest was for life only, died.

Hugh's son William was also a Jacobite but died before the '45 Rebellion. He was followed by a son of the same name who married Frances Sobieski the daughter of Christopher Ince of Ince-in-Makerfield.

A son William Ince Anderton who followed in 1811, acquired the manor of Euxton. This was the first time the Anderton's had held the manor although they had been resident in the locality from the late fifteenth century.

The first to be mentioned was Hugh Anderton of Euxton who built Euxton Hall. He was a younger son of Oliver Anderton of Anderton who was murdered by his wife in 1466. Hugh had a daughter Margaret who was betrothed in 1508 to Nicholas Rigbye heir to Harrock.

The present Euxton Hall was built in 1850 on the site of a hall built in 1769.

NOTED PAPISTS

Apart from their zealous support of the Divine right of kinds, the Anderton's were a noted Catholic family. Their name appeared quite early on the recusancy rolls, and in 1586, Alice Anderton, a widow, was sued for non-payment of £260 in such fines.

Dawbers Lane

Several members of the family entered the church, and the Venerable Robert Anderton of Douay, who died for the faith in the Isle of Wight in 1586, is said to be one of them. Thomas Anderton served as a Benedictine monk with the English Mission until his death in 1672. Three of his brothers were monks, one a Fransiscan.

The Molyneux family were also Catholic and Runshaw, which goes back to the early fifteenth century, was held by the Farnworth family, a number of whom became Benedictine monks.

CLAIMED THE CHURCH

In the light of this it is not surprising to find that in such a neighbourhood, the church, which began as a chapel of Leyland, was closed soon after the Reformation and used only for the mass when mission priests called at the village. Sir Robert Molyneux is generally credited with having rebuilt the chapel in 1513. At any rate, the initials on the datestone over the west door are said to be his.

The vigorous religious reforms of the commonwealth changed things, of course. In 1650 the church had its own minister, Mr. Seth Bushell, who later became vicar of Preston. He is believed to have been a member of the family who were landowners in Euxton for centuries. Spout House in Washington Lane was theirs and the estate was used in the endowment of Gossnargh Hospital founded by Dr. Bushell.

After the restoration, the Molyneux family claimed return of the church as their property, and it was not until forty years later, that the church of England got it back, in a rather sorry condition without pulpit of pews.

Thomas Armetriding Vicar of Leyland provided an endowment gave £200 and there was also a grant from Queen Anne's Bounty. The living continued in the gift of the family and James Armetriding was incumbent from 1774 to 1788.

The Armetridings were a well known Euxton family, taking their name from part of the Yarrow which originally meant "Hermit's Riding" or clearing. William Armetriding had land there in 1294.

The hall which was the home of the family is one of the oldest buildings in the district.

During the 18th century Catholic Worship was at Euxton Hall, and when a chapel was built by public subscription in 1817 it was in the grounds. It was purchased by William Ince Anderton in 1865, when a new Church of St. Mary was built. In the south transept of this church it is the Anderton chapel.

The Euxton C.E. School goes back to 1759. It was built by John Longworth, who acquired the manor from the Molyneux family. Rebuilding took place in 1837, and in 1851 it was recorded that there were 97 scholars of whom "13 were taught free."

CHAPTER ELEVEN

CHARNOCK'S CENTURIES OF FAITH

Charnock is thought to be an old form of 'Yarrow' which itself may derive from the Celtic 'Garwo' (rough). The river is 'rough' in places, particularly over its rocky bed in the hills. The theory is supported by the fact that the river flows through Heath Charnock (one Charnock Gogard) and makes a semi-circle round Charnock Richard. Both places are presumably named from one river.

Charnock Richard is supposed to have got its distinguished name from Richard de Charnock, who held half the manor in early days. He is first mention in 1242, but the family had been landholders in Charnock before then. Richard's father, Adam de Charnock, had been fined for supporting Prince John in the absence of Richard 'Lion Heart' on Crusade.

The Charnocks were in trouble again in 1315, when Charnock Richard was a rallying place for the rising against Thomas Earl of Lancaster. Robert Charnock lost his life at Preston but Adam Charnock was pardoned by the king.

The family also held Astley, and Robert Charnock, who is credited with building Astley Hall in 1577, made his home there with the first of his five wives.

As Charnock Richard (like Heath Charnock) was in Standish Parish, Robert took a prominent part in the rebuilding of Standish Church in 1585.

The family was strong Catholic and Robert himself was outlawed, possibly because of some association with his younger brother, John, who was put to death at Tyburn in 1586 as one of the Babington conspirators. The plot had been to assassinate Elizabeth and put Mary Stuart on the throne, but John's part must have been passive since he was allowed to die on the rope before being drawn and quartered – an act of mercy in those barbarous times.

'NEST OF RECUSANTS'

Queen Elizabeth must have heard of Charnock Richard. The other half of manor, held by Richard Hoghton who was also a Catholic adherent. Blessed Edmund Campion, who died for the faith in 1581, was forced on the rack to confess the names of those who had given him shelter and among those he mentioned was Richard Hoghton of Park Hall. But from books and other possessions he left behind at the hall it is assumed he made his home there.

Christ Church, Charnock Richard, a memorial to a young man's faith and determination.

The Alms Houses at Charnock Richard—a memorial to the family who won the village, its school and church.

Chaplains were maintained at Park Hall for two hundred years, and the first one, Blessed Lawrence Johnson, was executed at Tyburn in 1892. Other chaplains included Fr. Richard Scholes, Fr. Fawcett Dom Richard Hoghton O.S.B., Fr. P. Acton, Fr. Edward Hoghton O.S.B., and Fr. E. A. Eastham O.S.B. The Hoghtons it will be seen, entered the priesthood themselves and two of the family are said to have become nuns.

In the light of this, is it hardly surprising that Canon Porteus should suggest in his "History of Standish" that Charnock Richard was a 'nest of recusancy in Lancashire' and that sometimes bowlers at the Bowling Green Inn, carried not woods in their bags, but weapons.

The Hoghtons like the Charnocks, also took the King's side in the Civil War. William Hoghton who succeeded Richard at Park Hall, was killed at the first battle of Newbury in 1643. Parliament lost no time in sequestering the estate but when it was sold in 1653, the purchasers were acting for the Hoghtons. At any rate, they were still in possession in 1664 when William's son, John recorded a pedigree. His son William was succeeded by a son John, who took the name and arms of Dalton of Thurnham, his mother's family. This family sold the estate in 1789.

PARK AND FAIR

The estate was specially valued because of its park, which gave it its name. This went back to 1284, when Henry I granted free warren to Henry de Lea, whose lands ultimately descended to the de Hoghtons.

The royal charter provided for a market day every Friday and an annual fair on the eve, the day, and the morrow of St. Nicholas (later changed to St. Botulph).

The estate included lands in Welch Whittle, Chorley, Euxton and Heskin, besides Charnock Richard.

Welch Whittle gets its name from the Walsh (or Waley) family of Aughton, who acquired it in the 13th century. Later it went to the Torbucks, who gave it to the Wrightingtons in 1365 for help in a family dispute. The Hoghton share, included the wooded valley known as Whittle Green. There used to be a water mill here driven from the three meres at the front of Park Hall.

Only one mere remains, but it is wide and deep. Tradition had it that it is really a delph from which Benedictine Monks, in 908 hewed the red stone from which the hall is mainly built.

This first hall was supposed to commemorate the resting place of St. Cuthbert in 643 during seven years journey in a stone coffin as protection against body snatchers.

The present building has had many additions, but some interesting timber is preserved in the structure. It also has a striking appearance, particularly from the motorway, which has separated it from what was once Henry de Lea's "free warren." The public footpath is preserved however. Carried over the motorway by a footbridge, this leads to a picturesque wood where it divides and one can go through open fields to Tunsteads or Crook Lane.

No. St. Cuthbert died in 687, and it was not until 875 that the coffin was taken from Lindisfarne.

Tan House Farm, Charnock Richard (opposite the Bowling Green Inn) has an occupational name. Tanning was a profitable trade, judging by the size of the house, which has a stone base and hand made bricks of sixteenth century building. A datestone 1695 bears the initials F.R.E. The F stands for Foster. The other letters are for Christian names.

PANORAMA

Tunsteads is the highest point of Charnock Richard and on a clear day the view of the surrounding countryside is magnificent. The estuary of the Ribble, the Fylde and most of its coastline, are easily seen to the north west. Towards the south is Harrock of course, and to the east the Pennine foothills.

Close by Tunsteads is Old Hall Farm, on the site of what was once the home of the Charnocks, but the cottage which marks the top of the hill was a lodge for a drive to Park Hall.

This was listed regularly by Mr. Henry Alison, whose great grandfather bought Park Hall in 1789. Mr. Alison was a remarkable man. He died aged 87, in 1915, having lived under four sovereigns, Georve IV, Victoria, Edward VII and George V.

He was fond of walking, so fond in fact that when his carriage went to Euxton station each morning and returned each evening, it carried only his briefcase. Mr. Alison walked!

A practising barrister for ten years, Mr. Alison himself served on the bench, but gave up the appointment at the age of 32, when he became first treasurer for the County Palatine of Lancashire. During the 55 years he was in office, he saw vast changes, including the coming into force of the Local Government Act of 1888, which established county councils by popular vote.

Bolton Green Farm was built in 1612 by a tanner name Lowe, His wife is said to have been one of the Charnocks. The family were well to do as evidenced by the size and build of the house and the Jacobean spindle staircase and figured ceiling. Near the kitchen chimney is a cavity which could have been a hiding hole. The Lowes were in occupation until late in the 19th centry, when on the marriage of a daughter, the house became the property of Sir John Drinkwater, Demster I.O.M.

POVERTY A CRIME

An insight into earlier local government is provided by the records of the meetings of ratepayers and overseers in Mr. Alisons own township. These go back to 1826, when chief concern seems to have been making grants of two or three shillings per week, or of clogs or clothing to people in distress. That the distress was genuine there can be no doubt, for in these times poverty was a crime and in some parishes paupers were expected to wear a large red or blue "P" on their outer clothing.

Charnock Richard had its own land, known as the "poor land," which was let to a tenant for the income. Apparently when the new railway was built it went through this land, for a minute of 1837 records "agreed that the railway should pay a yearly rent of the whole poor land, and so do what they think proper for the other of their own profit."

In spite of this income, it was still necessary to levy a rate. Thus when Mr. Knagge was appointed molecatcher in 1839, at £4 10s. per year, a rate had to be levied to pay him.

At the same time John Rutter was appointed constable, an office he gave up a year later to become Guardian of the Poor. The office of constable was not popular. Property qualification was required to fill it and this reduced the number of candidates. In some townships eligible men paid quite big sums to keep out of the office!

James Sumner, the new constable, evidently needed inducement, for with John Green he was made surveyor of the highways at £3 per year. Eighteen years later James Sumner, having held various offices, became Assistant Overseer at £12 10s per year.

John Green and Richard Barrow were surveyors for a few years, then Richard Barrow was appointed on his own at £10 a year in 1845, when it was also agreed unanimously that he "keep the interest of the money in his hands, whatever it might be, towards defraying his expenses of journeys and such like belonging to the same."

TOWN CLERK

A name that appears from time to time in the records is that of Thomas Cowling. If it refers to one man, he served nearly 40 years! He had various offices including chairman, church warden, road surveyor, assessor, but his signature appears with the minutes of the first meeting over the title "town clerk".

Presumably he got the job because he could write. At any rate, some of the members of the committee marked their names with a cross. Later, the minutes were kept by Thomas Townley Parker, who made a very neat job of them too.

Representative of the family who had inherited the Charnock half of the manor through the Brooke's he resided at Charnock Richard at Alison Hall, and presided at parish meetings for seven years.

Although such titles as churchwardens and sidesmen were used most of the meetings were held on Charnock Green or at different houses in the township.

This must have had its complications, as when John Rosbottom wanted the parish to make up a road to his colliery. The meeting of ratepayers was held at his house in Charnock Green and Mr. Rosbottom himself seconded the motion, moved by one Mr. Whittle. Even so the redoubtable John Rutter was not overawed and his amendment "that the road be not mended at the expense of the township," was carried by 58 votes to 15.

About this time, 1841, Charnock had three coal miles, Railway, Charnock, and Park Hall. The "mountain coal" was of high quality and considered to be the most accessible in the Lancashire coal field. This no doubt saved the parish funds by providing employment, and the many field paths in the district which now make pleasant walks, were originally to enable folk to get to work.

Park Hall has been built at various periods. The mere at the front is said to be a delph from which the stone was obtained.

OPPOSITION

So far as highways were concerned, the chief interest of the overseers was to save money. How else could they get away with a highway rate of fourpence and sometimes sixpence, even when contracts for paving were let at three half pence a yard?

According to W. E. Tate ("The Parish Chest"), practically the only way to secure the repair of a road was the indictment in a criminal court of the inhabitants of the parish. This was done apparently as recently as 1921.

In Charnock Richard a public meeting on October 4th, 1841, decided that the surveyor should defend an indictment against the inhabitants for not repairing a lane called Bolton Green Lane, "beginning at the house of William Mosscrop and extending to the dwelling house of James Sumner and containing in length 1,232 yards and in breadth five yards."

The opposition is all the more remarkable because Bolton Green was one of the principal hamlets of the township. The lane, presumably the one now called Back Lane, was the direct route to Eccleston Green via Red Lane. Almost directly opposite was the road to Chorley, German Lane. The Wigan-Preston (South of Yarrow) Trust Road crossed between the two lanes as the A49 does today.

At the entrance to Back Lane on the left hand side was the police station (Could it have been the residence of James Sumner?) Further along as there is today, was the principal house, Bolton Green, built in 1612 by Ralph and Margery Lowe, whose initials are carved on the date stone. Leading off to the right was Mill Lane the road to Armetryding Mill. It was down here that a house was used for storing supplies for Government troops marching north, to suppress the 1715 Jacobite rising at Preston. The house now in ruins, was known as Commisary Farm ever after.

90

Commissary Farm

All this goes to show that the Lane in dispute had long established public use, but the inhabitants at large were not prepared to maintain it. They were not exceptional, so what must have been the state in the rest of the country!

Mr. Alison in his long service of treasurer saw all this change and played his part in developing services which not only meant more and better roads, but took care of education, and welfare of the sick and aged, until the turnover was several million pounds yearly.

Yet he found time to serve on his own parish council being chairman at its formation in the 1890's.

Long before that, the local overseers had found a vestry at last, for on March 25th, 1862, they had met in the then new Charnock Richard Parish Church, after which they adjourned to the schoolroom.

A TEMPLE IN HIS NAME

Both the church and the school owe their existence to the energy and persistence of one of their members, James Darlington, a local colliery owner.

At the age of 14, James had persuaded his father to let him conduct a young men's Bible class in a cottage.

At 25, he wrote in his diary "God helping me with health, life and prosperity. I will yet build a Temple to His Name."

The school came first. Two cottages in Charter Lane was opened for this purpose in 1856. On August 9th, 1858 the new school was opened, and the following months was "crowded with nearly 300 out of a population of 800."

In November, Mr. Darlington wrote in his diary "What next? Surely this is the shadow of the church and in it are the pastor's flock."

But a hard struggle lay ahead. There was opposition from the Vicar of Coppull, who did not want Charnock to have a separate ecclesiastical parish, and from the Squire (Mr. Alison's father). All this was somehow overcome and Mr. Darlington wrote in his diary "How faith removes mountains."

Christ Church was dedicated by the first Bishop of Manchester, the Rt. Rev. James Prince Lee on September 14th, 1860. first wardens were James Darlington and Mr. Alison.

Mr. Alison, who afterwards never missed more than two Sunday's attendance a year until his death in 1915, ceased to be a warden the following year. The parishioners elected Mr. Thomas Cowling as people's warden in his stead. Could this be the ubiquitous Mr. Cowling "town clerk"?

In September the same year, Mr. Darlington married Fanny Radcliffe in the church where she had laid the foundation stone two years before. In 1897 she gave the lych gate to mark the diamond jubilee of Queen Victoria, but the dedication on September 26th became a memorial service, for Mrs. Darlington had died three days before.

The date of her death is carved in stone on the beautiful almshouses built to her memory in 1898.

Her other memorial is her last message delivered from the pulpit just after her death. "She thought of you as her friend and loved you and trusted to see you again," the preacher said.

So there we have it, Charnock Richard the "nest of recusancy", keeping the flame of Catholic faith alive. Charnock Richard the mining village, where with the same inspiration a church and school were built upon faith.

CHAPTER TWELVE

HISTORY LIVES HERE

When the Charnocks rode from Charnock Richard to Astley they would most likely take what is now German Lane to cross the River Yarrow at the ford near Common Bank.

From here they would follow roughly the west bank of the river Chor to Astley Hall.

This is not merely conjecture. Southport Road as we know it did not exist. In fact as recently as a century ago Balshaw Lane, Euxton, was joined to Ackhurst by a drive with a lodge at the sharp bend at what is now known as Washington Lane. Furthermore there are still indications in Astley Park of a road which continued from Common Bank.

This would be high above the charming black and white lodge at Ackhurst which in spite of its antique appearance is of fairly modern origin.

It is said that a fire at Charnock Hall was the reason for Robert Charnock moving to Astley. The only clue as to when this was is an old stone found in the grounds bearing the inscription 1577 R.I.C. This is taken to mean that Robert Charnock was engaged in building somewhere around 1577 soon after his marriage to Isobel daughter of Sir William Norris of Speke.

Before that of course, there was a hall already in in existence at Astley which had probably been occupied by the Charnock younger sons. For me it will always be the black and white gable fronted house facing the lake. It was extensively restored in 1875, but its appearance is a perfect example of the 15th Century manor house with north and south wings and a central hall. What does it matter if new materials have been used so long as the shape is retained?

THE COURTYARD

Perhaps Robert Charnock and his bride went to live there following their marriage. Then he started building the hall round the courtyard with an entrance to the north. Much of this remains round the back of the main building. It has been restored with great care by Chorley Corporation and very charming it is.

Robert Charnock certainly needed commodious premises. He married five times and had numerous children.

Some of the old half-timbered hall shows its face in the west. Note the graceful Chimneys. This part has been restored by the Corporation.

His son and heir by Isobel Norris was Edward Charnock who went to Rivington School. There is a theory that this may have inspired building of Chorley Grammar School in 1611. At any rate Robert Charnock played a prominent part in that venture, supplying all the bricks!

Unfortunately, Edward, who was something of a scholar, died at Oxford — it is said from a surfeit of cherries.

In consequence when Robert died in 1616 he was succeeded by younger son Thomas, to whom he left "my gold ring with arms engraved upon it...to remain an heirloom."

Thomas had married Bridget, daughter and heiress of John Moleyneux, of Barton on Irwell. The lady was a considerable heiress and this may have resulted in further extensions at Astley. One suggestion is that the entire front of the hall then consisted of a great hall of timber and plaster with one oriel at the west end and a minstrel gallery at the other. This was rebuilt and raised another story with the two oriels which give the hall its present striking appearance.

Mr. Herbert Cescinsky in his report on Astley to Chorley Corporation suggests that these alterations were the work of old Robert Charnock in 1616. Canon Porteus found this difficult to follow because this was the year of Robert Charnock's death. The Victoria County History states that the alteration may have been the work of Thomas Charnock but was more likely that of his son, Robert.

Young Robert Charnock was 11 at the time of his grandfather's death. He became a noted soldier, being a captain of both sieges of the Earl of Derby's seat at Lathom House in 1644 and 1645.

At one of these engagements he is said to have lost an eye and although his portrait (No. 32) shows him with two there is a definite cast in the right eye which could have been caused by a musket ball. He may, of course, have been sensitive about the injury which earned him the nickname of "one eye".

Anyhow, the balding man with the pointed beard in the picture looks in his middle forties which was his age four years after the last seige of Lathom.

Perhaps the picture was painted on his marriage to Alice Farington of Worden, in 1649. He would then just be recovering from his troubles following the sequestration of his own estate by Parliament.

He had been allowed to succeed his father who had died in May, 1648, on payment of a fine of £260 — a lot of money in those days.

The visit of Cromwell to Astley must have taken place only a few weeks later, in the August.

HARDLY SLEPT A WINK!

There is some scepticism about this. Why should the Roundhead General choose to spend the night at the house of a Royalist Captain. who could hardly be in the best of humour having so recently been mulcted of a heavy fine.

Moreover, Cromwell had just driven a wedge between Sir Marmaduke Langdale's army at Ribbleton Moor and the Duke of Hamilton's at Walton-le-Dale had done such a bloody battle at Preston that though superior in numbers, the Duke's forces fled overnight to Wigan.

Cromwell himself said he slept in the field but that may have referred only to his men. He was however, in hot pursuit of the Royalist force and there was a skirmish at Chorley. If he slept at Astley, it could not have been for very long!

All the same, tradition dies hard and it is sometimes more true than what is written. People who put pen to paper usually had an axe to grind and did not hesitate to make the facts fit their purpose.

There is this about it to. If the Charnocks had not been flattered by the visit how could the tradition have started? After all, it was a custom to call rooms after distinguished visitors. At Alice Farington's home at Worden there is a whole Derby Wing. At Astley there is a Cromwell Room and in another room altogether a Cromwell Bed.

How the two became separated has mysified people for some time. Were the family so proud of the bed once occupied by the Lord Protector, they put it in a better room at the front? Or does the room answer the puzzle of who carried out the seventeenth century rebuilding?

Of course, there was good reason to move the bed even if Cromwell hardly slept at all. It was the best bed in the house. Canon Porteus describes it as a "handsomely carved fourposter emblazoned with the Charnock arms." It may go back to 1590 and is "the finest specimen of its age which has escaped destruction and would be among the most treasured possessions of a national museum."

It looks therefore as if Cromwell was given the best bed whether he hardly slept here at all.

He also left behind a pair of boots and later sent a portrait (the date is 1653). Now the custom of sending presents in return for hospitality was widespread. The Faringtons had a whole collection of Derby portraits at Worden. There is also the fact that in the year of Cromwell's supposed visit General Ashton's Brigade gave £86 to provide for a schoolmaster to teach grammar at the Chapel in Chorley, a pretty sure sign they were quartered in the town.

The portrait of the Protector (23) still hangs in Astley and although the line of his mouth is stern and the eyes watchful and alert, this is the face of a man who could be a philosopher or a priest. The same qualities are evident in the portrait of Robert Charnock. Perhaps when the two got together they found much in common though they had been on different sides. Perhaps they sat up half the night having a good natter as old soldiers do!

The old manor would have looked like this. The house overlooking the lake.

PURITAN DIVINE

Another indication that people were not so divided as historians would have us believe is the full length painting (14) of a sobre gentleman robed in brown, wearing wooden soled shoes. The features are unmistakenly those of a Charnock and if they are as is suggsted, those of Stephen Charnock, grandson of old Robert, he was a Puritan Divine. A scholar at Oxford and Cambridge he was a noted preacher and writer and resided for a time at Dublin with Henry Cromwell, son of Oliver.

According to Canon Porteus however, he died in 1860 two years earlier than the date of the portrait.

Still it is nice to think that even in a family so Catholic as the Charnocks "blood was thicker than water" and they could show proudly a portrait of a dinstinguished cousin though he was a Puritan.

JACOBITE PLOTTER

His nephew by the way was Robert Charnock a vice-president of Magdalen College in 1688.

He followed the Charnock tradition and took orders in the Catholic Church, but was also said to have been a captain and to have agreed to take part in an attack on William III on his return from hunting in Richmond Park in 1696. This particular Jacobite plot was discovered and Robert was executed at Tyburn a month later.

There was also Job Charnock who founded Calcutta, and John Charnock who wrote on naval affairs in the eighteenth century.

Unfortunately, the only other Charnock on view besides Stephen, is Robert the last of the male line at Astley. Not even his daughter Margaret is there. That is a pity. She was a remarkable woman.

Her first husband was Richard Brook son of Sir Peter Brooke of Mere.

The wedding in 1666, the same year as the Great Fire of London, is commemmrorated in the fine cealings at Astley. The arms of Brooke and those of Charnock are displayed over the fireplace of the great hall.

The Charnock arms are quartered with Molyneux, a connection of which the Charnocks were still proud.

Margaret Charnock bore her husband six sons and six daughters. She lived to be a great age dying in 1744, which would make her well over 90. Her second husband was John Gillibrand of Lower Chorley Hall who predeceased her in 1732. As a non juror in 1718, he registered his estate in Astley and Charnock.

SHERRIF OF TWO COUNTIES

Her first husband Richard Brooke is portrayed (8) stroking a dog. He is a cavalier in appearance and the long dark hair seems to be his own. He was a second son of Sir Peter Brooke who is also shown (6). He looks a bit standoffish but then he was High Sherrif of both Lancashire and Cheshire.

Although he came from Mere in Cheshire, he settled down at Astley and is buried in the chancel at Chorley Parish Church.

Peter Brooke the eldest son who succeeded Richard is a dark supercilious young man (11) according to his portrait. His wife (7) has a homely oval face and striking hair.

Peter died in 1721 without issue and was succeeded by his brother Thomas (13) a periwigged gentleman who was painted in middle-age and consequently looks older than his father, Richard Brooke, who was portrayed as a young man.

Thomas married Margaret Wharton of London in 1716 when her portrait (5) was probably painted showing a woman of rare beauty both in colour and shape and with exquisite hands. Even in a portrait of her as an older woman (9) the beauty is still there. It is not surprising to find she had two beautiful daughters. Jane (1) though not as lovely as her mother has much of her charm.

Elizabeth (20) is slightly prettier and has a roguish look in her eyes. A single string of pearls indicates a young woman of good taste.

Sons Richard and Peter Brooke who succeeded to Astley in turn are not depicted. Peter who married Susanna Crookhall of Clifton died in 1876 leaving a son Peter who died a year later. This Peter was succeeded by his sister Susanna who is shown on one portrait (24) as a lovely lady with cupid bow lips, a retrousse nose and hair slightly auburn.

More half-timber work in Astley—the courtyard restored by the Corporation. The beam below the upstairs windows on the left carries the date 1600.

POPULAR SQUIRE

This would be at the time of her marriage at Croston in 1787 to Thomas Townley-Parker. He died seven years later, aged 34, but had already been High Sheriff of Lancashire.

His portrait (30) shows him as a charming man, the popular type of squire. He was evidently fond of hunting and a painting (17) depicts his horses and dogs. His heir and successor, Robert Townley Parker, was an infant when his father died but resembles him in a portrait (31) when he was 17.

He has the same pleasant smile, the same broad forehead, but he gets his auburn hair from his mother. He also became High Sheriff of Lancashire and Deputy Lieutenant and was M.P. for Preston. He died aged 86.

'DREAM OF FAIR WOMEN'

Thomas Townley-Parker had two daughters. Susan (2) is easily the loveliest in this dream of fair women which Astley gallery largely is. She has her father's expressive eyes, her mother's curls and a generous smiling mouth. Aged 23, she married Francis Rich Price of Briny-Pis, of Flintshire. She died two years later.

Her younger sister Ann, is also portrayed (4) and although she has the same features and is indeed dressed the same she does not create the same impression as Susan.

Ann when she was 22 married John B. Clegg, of Withington and Gayton, Chester, who became High Sherriff of Chester three years later.

The mother of this family lived to the ripe old age of 90, dying in 1852. She was then Lady Hoghton having married Sir Phillip Bold Hoghton, of Hoghton, and borne him an heir, Sir Henry Bold Hoghton, seventh baronet, and a daughter.

It was Lady Hoghton who opened Park Road in 1822 on her way to Preston Guild.

It is as Lady Hoghton perhaps, after Sir Phillip's death that she is depicted in another portrait (21). In spite of her sombre clothes and a wrinkle here and there, she has not greatly changed. Her mough is straighter perhaps but there is still the roguish look in her eye. She must have been quite popular even in her old age. She was a lover of Astley and was specially proud of the Flemish tapestry which she insisted on dusting herself.

A remarkable woman, she bore heirs to two noted families. Her son, Sir Henry Bold Hoghton became the eighth baronet. Whilst through another son, Thomas Townley Parker who died in 1906, Astley and Cuerden descended to the latter's nephew Reginald Arthur Tatton.

Mr. Tatton, who gave the hall and some acres surrounding it to Chorley Corporation in February, 1922, as a war memorial, is commemorated in a fresco in the main hall.

99

Other pictures at Astley have family associations. That of Charles I and his family (3) though it may seem to run counter to Cromwell and the Puritan Divine was to be expected in the house of a Royalist family. There is also a portrait of Sir Matthew Hale (25) chief justice during the reign of Charles II which bears token to the fact that many Charnocks like Robert, father of Stephen, were lawyers.

Even hand painted panels of sailors, soldiers and monarchs from Tamarlane to William, Prince of Orange and including Elizabeth I and Philip of Spain, would seem to show a family trend!

One wonders if the leather covered travelling chest bound with metal (circa 1665) was used by Richard Brooke and Margaret on their honeymoon in 1666 — if they had one.

The oak banqueting table from Entwistle Hall recalls that the Townley Parkers were a noted family in East Lancashire. Then there is the showpiece of Astley, the suffleboard, 23½ft. long which seems to prove that the Brookes must have added the Long Gallery on to the top floor. This game, which was played by sliding metal weights from one end of the table to the other, required a good deal of skill and sometimes large sums of money changed hands.

No gentleman's mansion was complete without one of these in the reign of the Merry Monarch and doubtless the Brookes had to have one.

The purpose of these notes, however, is not to catalogue the historical content of Astley which is a treasure trove in this respect, but to show how some of these at least bring life to what for many of us have merely been names.

PARK WITHOUT FEAR

What is true of the hall is true of the park. A painting (27) of an Astley Hall of red brick shows the Nab and Parish Church out of perspective, but the formal gardens did exist and must have been very fine indeed. Even now one can think of fine gentlemen and ladies in the gay costumes of bygone days, strolling the terrace by the lake.

But the charm that induced Sir Peter Brooke to leave the beautiful estate he had purchased at Mere, and Sir Philip Hoghton to forsake his ancestral home a few miles away, would be the woods and the beautiful parkland which gave Astley a situation without peer, even among stately homes.

There is also the river. Bottled up by now by a culvert almost from its source in Cabbage Hall Fields, the Chor escapes joyously to freedom in the park where it winds through the woods under quaint arched bridges of stone and in season receives homage from snowdrops, daffodils and bluebells which grow in profusion on its steep banks.

Today the lake has stolen the River Chor's glory, and they even say that besides being the fishpond it was a mill dam. But the Chor drove many mills in its time, and I like to think there was a mill in Astley woods where I once found a millstone nearby. And then I can learn on the bridge like the miller did 400 years ago, and think that history lives here.

The numerals in brackets relate to portrait numbers at Astley Hall.

The familiar face of Astley Hall. The gutter on the left bears the initials B.P.S. for Peter and Susan Brooke and the date 1752.

CHAPTER THIRTEEN
THE LOVELY VALLEY

Before the River Chor joins the Yarrow, it fills the lodges of Chorley Bleach Works. Surrounded by the trees of Big Wood and Copper Works Wood, these have a pleasant lakeland appearance.

Prior to the housing development of post-war years, the walk from here alongside the river used to emerge at the Walletts, so called after the wood of that name. There were also the extensive Gillibrand woods and open fields.

Gillibrand Hall, however, still stands on a prominence which makes it easily seen from as far away as Charnock Richard. It is expressive of a period which produced many imposing buildings. It was in fact built for £15,000 in 1808, in replacement of a much older building described by a contemporary as "fortresslike."

As early as 1733, the Gillibrands had been insisting that Gillibrand Hall as it had really been known, was really Chorley Hall. There may have been some justification for the claim.

The Manor of Chorley became divided about 1330 when Margaret Banastre (she had been three times married) died. She left four daughters as heirs. These were Katherine, wife of Sir John Harrington; Alice, wife of Robert de Shireburn; Agnes, wife of Robert de Horncliffe; and Joan, who left a son, Thomas de Arderne.

There was some litigation and William de Ferrers of Groby, whose family acquired Chorley immediate lordship about 1250, seems to have recovered the Arderne part, as settlement of an hereditary claim. At any rate when he died in 1371, he possessed half of the manor.

SOLE LORD

This half went to the Audlems as payment for finding a bailiff at the Hundred Court and after forfeiture of Sir Thomas Gray in 1484, it was held by the Crown who gave it to the Stanleys. They eventually sold it in 1597 to the Rigbys.

The Harrington and Shireburn parts were merged in 1574 when Sir Richard Shireburn of Stoneyhurst acquired the Harrington part which had come into the possession of Lord Mounteagle.

This half of the manor descended to Thomas Weld of Lulworth of the family who gave Weld Bank its name. It was acquired in 1825 by Thomas Gillibrand who had inherited the other half which had been acquired by John Gillibrand in 1700.

Gillibrand Hall, built in 1808, replaced an older building, claimed to be Chorley Hall. The entrance gate in Gillibrand Walks, near where St. George's Vicarage now stands, was removed to save Astley Park main entrance. Gillibrand Hall is now run by the Congregation of La Sagesse, as a home for girls.

Thomas, who thus became sole Lord of the Manor of Chorley was a descendant of Richard Chorley of Chorley Hall through the latter's daughter Elizabeth (died 1662) who had married a John Gillibrand.

The claims to the title Chorley Hall may thus appear to have been a family feud, though the Harringtons are said to have made their home at Lower Chorley Hall.

In any case, Gillibrand is an old name in Chorley, being mentioned amongst the landholders as early as 1430. The family were strong Catholic and at least two became Jesuit priests, one of them being well-known locally for his Mission at Slate Delph in Wheelton.

Thomas Gillibrand the builder of the present Gillibrand Hall, forsook his church however. According to one authority, he quarelled with the priest for refusing to allow him to smoke his pipe in chapel. As a result, the family became Protestant. Just before he died, 1828, he gave the town its Market Hall.

His son, Henry Hawarden Gillibrand, changed his name to Fazakerley in 1815 on inheriting the Fazakerley Estate.

He is said to have fought a duel with T. B. Crosse of Shaw Hill in 1832, but neither party was injured. It was about this time that much of Gillibrand estate was being worked for coal.

Henry's son and heir was in fact killed in an accident underground. As a result the estate passed to the Westby family and was later sold.

The purchaser in 1881 was the late Henry Rawcliffe.

The Rigby's who held half of the Chorley Manor until 1700, were close neighbours of the Gillibrands.

They were also Catholics. Edward Rigby of Burgh, a free-holder and Justice of the Peace in 1600 was described as 'evil given in religion' and 'no communicant – his wife never at church.'

Similar strictures were passed on Alexander Rigby of Burgh, who was also a principal landowner in Duxbury.

ON THE KING'S SIDE

In the Civil War, Alexander Rigby of Burgh was Commissioner of Array on the King's side and his eldest son Edward is said to have died at Bolton in the royalist cause.

Edward's son Alexander was a coronet under Sir Thomas Tyldesley in 1651. Sir Thomas was killed in the battle of Wigan Lane on August 25th, 1651, and Alexander, when High Sheriff in 1679, erected a monument to him, near the spot where the fine old soldier received his last wound.

So that when Chorleians pass this monument in Wigan today (it's not 200 yards past the infirmary), let them remember a Chorley man put it there.

The barn at Gillibrand Hall Farm carries a datestone 1669 and is subject to a protection order by the Ministry of Works. The door contains holes said to have been caused in a shooting affray.

There was another Alexander Rigby in the Civil War. Col. Rigby who was on Parliament side. This family came from Kirkham and the colonel's mother was an Asshaw from Flixton – a member of the Hall o' th' Hill family of Heath Charnock.

In the attempt to relieve the royalist garrison at Thurland Castle in 1643, Mr. Alexander Rigby of Burgh (not the coronet) led the royalist force from Cartmel, but was severely beaten by the Colonel of the same name!

Following Civil War sequestrations and fines the family made their principal home at Layton near Blackpool, where they also had possessions.

The son of Alexander of Burgh the coronet, also Alexander, prospered in commerce and became High Sheriff in 1691 and was knighted in 1696.

Then disaster struck. One of Sir Alexander's ships captured a French vessel in 1696 and the Grand Duke of Tuscany treated it as piracy and imprisoned the captain. Sir Alexander had to pay a heavy fine which brought about his ruin. He was a prisoner in the Fleet in 1713, and later the estates were sold and came into possession of Mathew Cragg, of Cammerton and Burgh, whose heiress married in 1744, Thomas Chadwick, son of John Chadwick of Birkacre.

The Chadwicks were prominent Catholics and had a chapel at Burgh Hall. The Rev. John Chadwick, fourth son of John Chadwick the elder, and brother of Thomas, founded Weld Bank Mission in 1774. The library and books from Burgh Hall were bequeathed to the mission.

The Chadwicks sold Burgh in 1824 to James Anderton, from whom it was purchased by John Thom in 1891.

Mr. Thom, a brilliant chemist, a colleague of scientist Professor Siemens and schoolfellow of the explorer, Livingstone, built up Birkacre print works into a large firm. This was the industrial zone of Chorley from early times.

EARLY TEXTILE MILLS

Canon Porteous points out that as early as 1423 a "walking" mill as well as a corn mill at Birkacre is mentioned. "Walking", he explains, was treading on cloth in a mixture of fullers earth to thicken it. The existence of a mill for this purpose suggests there were textile mills in the locality.

There was also coal mining as disused shafts and traces of old tramways confirm, and the name Higher Forge indicates there must have been iron works too.

The Chadwicks were industrialists and encouraged there enterprises. One of these was the spinning mill which Arkwright and his partners erected there to use his new machinery.

In October, 1779, however, a mob of "2,000 and upwards" attacked the place. They were repulsed, two being killed and eight wounded and taken prisoner. They returned the next day with reinforcements and smashed the machinery and set the buildings on fire.

The York Militia under Sir George Saville arrived too late. It is said they had tarried at the Eagle and Child, in Standish.

One of the oldest buildings in Chorley, 15th century Lower Burgh Hall. William Crooke, who re-built Coppull Parish Church in 1654, lived here.

Water power made this part of Yarrow Valley an industrial centre. A view of the weir which diverts the river along the lodges for which Birkacre is now famous.

The works was rebuilt in 1781 and leased to the calico printers Bolton and Co., who however, failed in 1782.

Various firms leased it, but no real progress was made until the arrival of Mr. Thom in 1852. In 1899 the family business was taken over one part by the Calico Printers and the other by the Bleachers' Association.

In the slump years both factories closed and have now been demolished. All that remains of past greatness is the lodges and waterfalls, a reminder that Yarrow's water power was why this place was chosen by industry at all. It was valued before then. In 1398 John de Coppull granted Robert de Burgh licence to make a mill pool and turn the course of the river.

Birkacre was divided into three parts in 1423, after the death of Robert Burgh, for his three daughters, Ellen wife of Ralph Molyneux, Margaret wife of Richard Ashton, and Alice wife of James Standish.

According to Canon Porteus, the Standish part is Lower Burgh, which was the home of the Crooke family who built Coppull Parish Church.

Alexander Rigby of Arley bought the other parts in 1561 about that time and the family came to live at Burgh.

THREE WAYS?

The division raises an interesting point about the wood called Drybones in the Whetstone Valley. One derivation of this term is "Three Ways" a name given to the cottage. Could it be this was the dividing point of the three estates?

Or was it merely someone trying to be funny about a valley called Whetstone?

Whatever it is, this bend in the river is one of the most picturesque parts of this lovely valley.

In a poem about it, poet historian John Wilson, wrote in 1903:

> But Drybones is the sweetest spot.
> Thou passed by O' Yarrow
> Though noble's hall adorn it not,
> No dwelling save a poor man's cot,
> Who beareth Adam's arms I wot,
> The gardener's spade and barrow.

In the Whetstone Valley, Drybones Wood — one of the Yarrow's beauty spots. The cottage, hidden partly by trees, was called "Three Ways", said to be a derivation of Dry Bones.

Burgh Hall Farm. The barn has a date stone 1729 and the initials L.C. which indicate it was built soon after the Craggs bought Burgh.

CHAPTER FOURTEEN

ROUND BY THE OLD MILL

Few things are so dear to the heart of an Englishman as the sight of corn mill with foaming current turning the paddles, and above the roar of the water, and rumbling from inside of the great revolving stones that turn the grain into flour.

There was such a mill at Duxbury, on the banks of the Yarrow and seventy years ago it inspired the following verse.

> The Eden of Lancashire some people say,
> Is a place they call Yarrow Bridge.
> If you go down that way on a fine Summer's day
> I am sure you'll agree that it is.
> It was down in that valley I met lovely Sally,
> Close by the rippling rill.
> An took her as far
> As a walk round the Carr
> Till we came to the Old Duxbury Mill.
> The water was rowling and Sally fro' Cowling
> Sang a song to the clock of the old water wheel.
> The miller was working, no time was he shirking
> Grinding his corn into flour and meal.
> The cock was a crowing, the brook was a flowing
> When I asked her to be mine,
> She said 'I will.'
> That was while I was strowling with Sally from Cowling
> Round by the Old Duxbury Mill.

The poet was Fred Dickenson, a miner, who lived in Tootell Street, and had the nickname of 'Oyster Fred' because of his spare-time occupation of selling oysters. He composed a number of poems and 'Sally from Cowling', the one quoted, was a favourite.

The mill, a four storey building, was demolished soon after the first world war. It was mentioned in documents as early as 1354 and in more recent times was worked by Joseph Sumner and Co., Mr. Thwaites, Messrs. Bentley and Trippett, and lastly by Nicholas Gillett and his son Richard. It had a thriving trade grinding oats for farmers for many miles around. A stone in the wall in which was embedded an iron ring for tethering horses, bore the date 1665.

High above the mill, for hereabouts the Yarrow Valley is deep, was Duxbury Hall in its wooded park, which still vies with Astley for the beauty annd variety of its trees.

The old mill at Duxbury. It was demolished soon after the first world war.

It was a stone faced building and lithographed drawings of the front showing deer in the foreground, and the southern side, appear in the County Palatine of Lancaster Section (Vol. 1) of "The Mansions of England and Wales." It was also noted for its spiral staircase of white marble.

When the hall and 541 acres was acquired from the Mayhew estated in 1932 by Chorley Corporation, the hope was expressed that although it was to be used for building development, the hall would be preserved.

Unfortunately this was not to be. The elaborate design included internal downspouts which when they leaked, did not show up the defect until too late.

This, together with the use of the hall for storing mining explosives during the war, produced a situation where the cost of repair was too great and the hall was demolished in 1952.

A PRIMITIVE HALL

Now all that remains, apart from a number of outbuildings is the old barn, built on six pairs of crooks resting on bases of stone.

John Wilson, the Chorley Historian, wrote in 1903, that it had been suggested this old barn may once have been a primitive hall itself.

"In the early ages of England country gentlemen's residences were on a much smaller scale than they are now. Master and men had meals at the same table – the salt cellar dividing them. The squire and his spouse had their bedchamber, the maidservants another, and the men slept in the common hall as best they might."

The chief historical interest of Duxbury however, was for the Americans who made frequent pilgrimages to the place and still do. Captain Myles Standish, the military leader of the Pilgrim Fathers, is supposed to hail from there. He called his home in New England, Duxbury, and claimed descent from the Standishes of Standish.

Canon Porteus who deals with matter fully in "Captain Myles Standish" (Manchester University Press 1920), points out that the estates to which Captain Standish laid claim were those of the Standish family of Ormskirk who also held land in the Isle of Man. Captain Standish also appears to have made the common mistake of thinking the Standishes of Duxbury and Standish were the same, when they were not.

It was on the occasion of the claim made in 1840 on behalf of the captain's descendants that defacement was alleged of the page in Chorley Parish Register, on which might have been expected to appear the date of Myles Standish,if he had been born in the parish. The register has, however, a number of defaced pages, through being stored in a damp place, and in any event, recent use of infra-red photography has failed to settle the question.

AT AGINCOURT

If Myles Standish felt he had been cheated out of his estate by the Standishes of Duxbury it was not the first time such an accusation had been made–nor the last.

The circumstances in which Hugh de Standish (said to be the son of Robert de Haydock, Rector of Standish) first acquired the manor are suspicious to say the least, for it was at a time when the owner, Henry de Duxbury, had been imprisoned at Lancaster for his part in the Banastre Rising of 1315.

Appeals were made by the Duxbury family, who had held land in Duxbury from early times, but the Standishes remained in possession, until 1898–adding considerablely to their estates lands including Heapey and Bradley.

Among the distinguished members of the family, were Sir Rowland who brought back from abroad, the reputed bones of St. Lawrence, which were given to Chorley Parish Church. Sir Rowland was a noted soldier who served under Henry V and Henry VI, and fought at Agincourt. He was slain at Gerberoy in 1434.

The redlic was given to the church by his brother, James, who succeeded him to the estate, on the formation of a chantry to say prayers for Sir Rowland, Dame Jane, his wife and other members of the family "their predecessors and successors."

Great beams of timber frame the old barn at Duxbury Hall, like the inside of a ship.

There was also a Duxbury Chapel at Standish Church, in which parish Duxbury was then situated. The building of this chapel is supposed to have been Thomas Standish, who is also thought to have rebuilt the hall in 1623. The hall was a brick building on a stone base, traces of which were to be seen in the cellars of the later hall.

The theory that it was built by Thomas is based on the fact that after a fire in the north wing on March 2nd, 1859, a stone was uncovered which bore the crest of achievements of Thomas Standish and his first wife Anne, eldest daughter of Sir Thomas Wingfield, of Letheringham, Suffolk.

The shield surmounted by two esquires helmets and the cock argent of Standish and the winged cap of Wingfield, was almost as elaborate as the one on the Standish pew placed in Chorley Parish Church in 1600 by Thomas's father, Alexander.

The Standishes had reason to show increasing interest in heraldy they had made alliances of well known families including the de Hoghtons, the Ashetons of Whalley Abbey, and the Faringtons of Leyland.

By a coincidence the year on the Duxbury stone was the one in which Anne Wingfield died.

Thomas married again, this time Anne Christopher of Whittingham, Suffolk and by her had three sons and four daughters.

Tom Standish, who took possession of the hall by force in 1812 claimed to be a descendant of one of these.

By the first marriage however, there were four sons and two daughters. The eldest son Thomas was a captain in the Leyland Hundred trained band, and on the royalist side, when a sniper from the church steeple at Salford shot him as he washed his hands outside his lodgings. That was in September, 1642.

The following month his father died. He had been M.P. for Preston for two years and was a zealous Parliamentarian.

TURNED PROTESTANT

Whether his son and heir had gone on the other side from conviction or the policy of having members of a family on both sides is not known. The Standishes of Duxbury by now, unlike the Standishes of Standish, were Protestant. This led to conflict between the two families, particularly where Jacobitism was concerned.

No mention is made of any further part played in the Civil War by the Standishes of Duxbury, though Captain Standish's younger brother Richard, was a colonel on the Parliamentary side.

There was, however, activity near the hall. When Hamilton's men were being pursued in August, 1648, it is thought that the Scots made a defensive position somewhere near Red Bank. In the skirmish at this place, Colonel Thornhaugh "when being without arms" is supposed to have been killed by a Scots lancer.

The Duxbury Hall of Frank Standish – copy of a lithographic drawing from 'Mansions in England.'

The bridge over the Yarrow at Red Bank, was of course important being on the common way north and south.

Years before in 1521 it was complained that James Standish of Duxbury had been levying a toll of 2d. for every 20 oxen or sheep that crossed, though it was not known by what right!

The common way would be more to the west than the present road which was built to relieve depression after the American War of Independence.

Captain Standish was without surviving issue and Col. Standish succeeded the father and also became M.P. for Preston.

His eldest son, also Richard, became the first baronet in 1677. He represented Wigan as a Whig from 1690 until his death in 1693—something that would bringhim into conflict with the Jacobite Standishes of Standish.

DETERMINED WOMAN

His wife was Margaret, daughter of Sir Thomas Holcroft, of Newchurch, and she seems to have been a very determined woman. When Peter Shaw, of Rivington, and George Smythe discovered deposits of lead on the Standish land in Anglezarke, she opposed the formation of a partnership to mine the strike. The venture was not successful until after Sir Richard's death in 1693, when it produced for Dame Margaret £20 to £25 a day. It was then alleged she wanted the whole advantage for herself and turned out the partners.

High court action followed, but though it went against her Dame Margaret won the day, having so wrecked the mines that the complainants gave up.

She was said to have 'turned the river (the Yarrow?) into the mines and cut up the engine and tools.'

Sir Richard's eldest son, Sir Thomas, who succeeded him, and became high Sheriff, revived the mining interest in 1721, when he leased to common land in Anglezarke for this purpose, near Black and White Coppice. The smelting mill was to be at a place called "Wharf" thought to be the origin of Warth Brook.

Sir Thomas's grandson, Sir Frank, the last baronet, was Tory M.P. for Preston. He also tried his luck at mining and between 1781 and 1787 production rose from four tons of lead per annum to more than 70 in the last two years.

Witherite used by Josiah Wedgewood in a secret process was also discovered in Sir Frank's time on Stronstrey Bank (the black outcrop behind Waterman's Cottage extending to Black Coppice). Previously the substance (barium carbonate) was supposed to have medical qualities and was used for rat poison!

Wedgewood's secret was not long preserved for one James Smithels was caught collecting the stuff, to export it to German procelain makers! Could he have given his name to the cottage called Smithels close by?

Oddly enough, an account published in 1835, suggests that Sir Frank did not do too well out of his mining. He "drove fresh shafts from the foot hills to the heart of the mine in order to carry off water, and enable men to work; but having engaged several sets of workmen who all conspired to defraud him, he became tired of the mining and in 1790, after having sunk some thousands of pounds in the undertaking, the work was again discontinued."

The goblet of glass "for a drink for the man what brings up the first coal."

SEIGE OF DUXBURY HALL

On Sir Frank's death in 1812, the lack of heir named Standish and the lapse of the baronety, caused a number of claimants to come forth.

One was a weaver, Tom Standish, who gathered together 100 colliers as supporters and took the hall by force at 5 pm. on June 4th, 1813.

The Governors of Preston House of Correction with a body of constables was sent with warrants to arrest the prisoners, but only found that Tom was now "Sir Thomas" and produced a family tree to prove it.

The constables not only failed to gain access, but were driven as far back as the Yarrow Bridge.

In the end the Dragoons arrived and took the whole garrison prisoners, "Sir Thomas" and five others were later sentenced for twelve months, so ended the Siege of Duxbury Hall."

Part of the Moat at Bretters (Old English for 'British').

DUXBURY RACES

Whilst "Sir Thomas" was waiting trial his friends used the park as a playground for various games. They also held Duxbury Races and Yarrow Bridge Fair.

A song at the time ran:–

> "From Wigan the constables brave did repair,
> To Duxbury Races and Yarrow Bridge Fair;
> To keep our true landlord our efforts did fail;
> They carried Sir Thomas to Lancaster Jail.
> But we'll fetch him back;
> He'll nothing lack.
> And in spite of lawyers and Master Frank Hall
> He shall ride in a carriage to Duxbury Hall."

Frank Hall was a great grandson of Margaret daughter of Sir Thomas Standish and Jane Turnour. A man of letters and a connoisseur he was responsible for the Duxbury Hall the lithograph drawings.

The older hall about 1828 was encased in stone. The pleasure gardens including the tunnel entrance to the bathing pool, would then be added. Frank Hall, who assumed the name of Standish, also filled the place with copies of pictures which formed the famous gallery, he is said to have bequeathed with his valuable library, to the King of France, in a pique, because he could not succeed to the baronetcy as well as the estate.

The motive may contain a grain of truth, but one fact stands out. Although he lived abroad Frank Hall Standish loved Chorley. When he died in Cadiz, according to his will, his body had to be conveyed to Chorley Parish Church for burial in the family vault.

The fulsome memorial in the chancel was not as some suspect, of his choosing. It was put there by William Standish Carr (also a great grandson of Margaret) who succeeded only by an instrument in the Will of Frank Hall Standish. This was in spite of bitterness in the claim in 1812.

On reflection, one cannot help feeling that Frank Hall Standish, of whom William Standish Carr had said "he has not a drop of Standish blood in his veins," was the noblest Standish of them all.

William Standish Carr who presumably gave his name to Carr Lane ultimately adopted the surname Standish and the estate continued in the family until September 1891, when it was sold to Mr. Philip Mayhew.

Once more there was a claimant from Wigan, this time William Hall, a retired coachman who with his son Charles broke into the hall and another siege started

The intruders were apprehended and charged with unlawful entry and punished.

OLD BRITISH

An interesting point raised by John Wilson in 'verses and notes' (A. Hill) is that the Standishes did not come in possession of Duxbury Hall themselves until 1623.

He suggests that they may have made their home at Bretters or Brettarghs, which before the construction of the railway and canal would be with easy access of the rest of Duxbury.

Brettargh is an old word for British meaning that there was a settlement of Britons at this spot, after the Anglican Invasion. There is still a moat at Bretters which may have surrounded a very old hall, perhaps the one known as "The Peel" (or castle) referred to in the Standish papers in the sixteenth century.

It was completely demolished, but there is a theory that much of the stone went to the rebuiling of Hall o' th' Hill in 1724, by Mr. Thomas Willis, M.P. for Wigan. His family had acquired Hall o' th' Hill sometime before Mr. Ellis Heyes who had suffered much in the Civil Wars by having both sides quartered on him in turn!

He had married in 1656 Kathleene daughter of Thomas Standish of Duxbury.

The final winding up of Duxbury was on March 23rd, 1934, when owing to boundary revision, the parish council held its last meeting. This took place in the Yarrow Bridge Inn (formerly the Standish Arms). In spite of the 1894 Act, which forbids meetings of public bodies in public houses, the council had always told the authorities had others who protested, that there was no other place with a public room in Duxbury.

So ended – as the report states – "a period of law breaking over the past 44 years without parallel in the country!"

Yet it had been quite a distinguished council. Electeed Guardian in 1868, Thomas Whittle had become Mayor of Chorley in 1884. He was the son of John Whittle who in 1840 had paid £8,000 for the Duxbury Pit – a shaft of which still exists near the site of the old mill.

The lifting of the first coal is commemorated on a glass goblet which was filled for the man who brought up the first piece of coal, and it is still a prized possession of John Whittle's great-grandson, Mr. Thomas Whittle of Lymm.

The piece of coal is treasured by a great-granddaughter, Mrs. A. Fairer, of "Littleholme," Chorley, who also has a pair of Standish lances bought by her father at the sale at Duxbury, in 1891.

To all this may be added a sentiment expressed in "The Chorley Guardian" in 1932. "The fact that Chorley Corporation have purchased Duxbury Hall and are planning to lay out the estate for building cannot efface such history as this."

This is where the stream from the water wheel entered the Yarrow at Duxbury Mill.

CHAPTER FIFTEEN

THE HUNTING GROUND OF KINGS

Just to the East of Yarrow Bridge, quite close to the old smithy, the River Yarrow is joined by Black Brook. This is not a new name brought about by industrial pollution, though the water of the stream is certainly cloudy. Black is an old word used of water in many places and oddly enough, Douglas, the name of the other river which flows from the hills, means black stream.

Black Brook begins in the moors near to Great Hill, and after making its contribution to Liverpool Corporation at the Goyt at White Coppice, which it crosses, it fills several lodges for Heapey Works. Emerging on the other side of the works,it pretty well follows its course, a much larger stream than the Yarrow. In fact the weir that used to divert water to te the mill race at Duxbury would be but a trickle without Black Brook.

It was on this account that some local still call it Weir Brook. As one of them told me "It is not Yarrow Bridge at all, but Weir Bridge—or if not that then Black Brook Bridge!"

For some reason however, there is a shyness about using the name Black Brook, and two factories not far from its banks are called after the Yarrow!

Yarrow is certainly a prettier name and in the days when coaches ran services between Chorley Moor, Bolton, Preston, Lancaster, Wigan and Southport (a seaside resort even then) the Yarrow Bridge Hotel the Yarrow Bridge Hotel was an important centre for travel.

De Quincey mentioned it in his 'Confessions of an Opium Eater.'

Originally it was on the bank of the river not far from the weir, the old road passing the front of the Doll House and crossing Carr Lane near the mission, continuing through Duxbury woods.

According to Dr. Aitken who made a survey for canals in the eighteenth century, the surface south of the Yarrow was 'pebble stones bruised with hammers with nothing to fill the intersticies.'

The North of the Yarrow Turnpike was opened in 1823 and the South of Yarrow in 1837 continuing along Wigan Lane instead of following the line of the present A6.

Sometime after that, the Yarrow Bridge Hotel moved and so presumably did the smithy, the buildings of which are still close by.

Eight arches span the valley of Black Brook, near Yarrow Bridge.

Stone mills and cottages give Cowling a 'Yorkshire' look.

'SHUTTLE SERVICE'

The coach traffic would keep both the inn and the smithy busy, until the coming of the railway from Bolton to Preston in 1846. Even then the coaches were not quite finished.

The valley of Black Brook had to be spanned with eight arches and these could not be finished before the permanent way. In consequence, for a time, north and south lines were linked by a coach service from Rawlinson Lane to Chorley!

Another old route which ought to be mentioned is Yarrow Gate. This also runs closer to the Black Brook than the Yarrow, but presumably the name is because of the connection with the Yarrow Turnpike.

A beautiful old farmhouse, near to the Bolton Road gives a clue to the route of this road. It is called Halliwells and my guess is that originally the lane followed the line of Yarrow Road, Eaves Lane, and Northgate to Halliwell Lane which joins the trunk road near the Water Tower on Chorley's northern boundary. It was not uncommon to name lanes after places a considerable distance away. Another example is Higher House Lane in Anglezarke.

In the case of Halliwell Lane oddly enough the new motorway will follow much of the line through Cabbage Hall fields. Who says history doesn't repeat itself?

CHORLEY SPA

Yet another lane from Yarrow Bridge is Hoggs Lane, which provides a short cut to Limbrick. It is said that to go along here one had to pay toll to a man called Hogg, who was bailiff to the Standish estate. He lived at Springfield House, which was built as a lodge for the keeper of the saline bath built by Mr. John Wilkinson. One of the springs that gave Springwood its name was found to have medicinal properties in 1847, and Yarrow Bridge thus had its spa.

The grounds of Springwood House were set out with ornamental gardens and ladies and gentry came in broughams and victorias to bathe and take the waters!

Another interesting set of buildings up Hoggs Lane was Tincklers Barracks. These were pulled down a few years ago, but how they got their name and whether they were headquarters for the old Volunteers, I could never discover. Perhaps they had something to do with the canal. That also follows the valley of the brook nobody owns.

The gentle curve between Duxbury and Cowling provides some of the best scenery on the entire canal.

Just past where Tincklers Barracks used to be, is Hall i' th' Wood, one of the oldest sites in Chorley. In 1561 the estate was sold by John Crosse to William Chorley. The younger members of the Chorley family may have lived there.

Once the Port of Chorley, Knowley Wharf has a deserted look.

Knowley Brow, known to the hundreds who flock to Anglezarke by way of Heapey Road. In the distance, Nine Arches Bridge, which carried the now discontinued Blackburn line.

GREAT REFORMER

It is at Cowling that the scene becomes really industrial. In some ways the grey stone mills and cottages in the valley give the impression of a Yorkshire mill village.

One of the mills was occupied in fact by a man who had been educated in Yorkshire at a 'Do-the-boys-hall' type school. He was none other than Richard Cobden, the free trade pioneer, whose name is inseperably linked with that of John Bright. ~La~

Richard and his brother Frederick were in the calico printing trade, but soon after making the venture at Chorley Richard entered the political field. This caused him to neglect his business and in spite of aid from friends, the mill passed from the hands of the family.

A bust of the famous man reposed however in Crosse Hall Mill until a few years ago. Another memorial to the Cobdens is Cobden Street off Eaves Lane.

MARRIED A CHORLEY

The mill used by the Cobden brothers was quite near to the aqueduct, which carries the canal over Black Brook. On the other side was Crosse Hall, the home of the Crosse family. They not only sold land to the Chorley's, but intermarried with them too. William Chorley (born 1565) married Elizabeth, daughter of John Crosse of Crosse Hall.

The bride's father, however, spent most of his time at Crosse Hall in Liverpool, of which city he was mayor in 1566.

Crosse Hall, Chorley, had a datestone 1697 and the initials of Thomas Crosse and his wife Mary Clayton of Adlington Hall. The building has been demolished but the barn which remains has some interesting arched windows which suggest it may have been used for religious purposes.

Like the Chorley's, the Crosses supported the Catholic cause in troublesome times, though later members of the family were Protestant.

Crosse Hall was forsaken in 1750, when Thomas Crosse married Sarah Ashburner of Preston, who was heiress to the estate formed at Shaw Hill.

Neighbours of the Crosse's were the Tootells, who acquired Lower Healey from the Andertons in 1599. They were another Catholic family and Christopher Tootell became a priest who although the vicar of Preston tried to secure his arrest, ministered at Lady Well Brindle for years. He was a noted author of devotional works.

In the Civil War, John Tootell took the side of the King and his estates were later sequestrated, then declared forfeit.

PARK RANGERS

In this valley, where history and industry dwell side by side and where mills take on the name of old halls, it is not surprising to find that the largest textile mill is close to a spot which for centuries was the home of the

Parkers. They got their name it is thought, from the occupation of the park ranger, when Healey was a royal park.

Hugh Parker and his wife Katherine are mentioned in 1443.

In 1480 James Parker of Bagganley had enemies who stole or destroyed his goods and maimed his cattle. They could not be caught so he appealed to the church who put a strong curse upon them. Above the seal of the Rural Dean of Leyland, a malediction was pinned to the doors of the local churches. It denounces as "accursed" those who had stricken the cattle of James Parker with an axe or a bill, also who took the horse of the said James out of Nab Wood and who smote a swine that it died, and also who stole any of his fish, hogs or cattle.

Evidently vandalism and pilfering were prevailent in those days, but there is an interesting theory that the culprits may have been Scots. They appear to have come further south than generally thought.

Bagganley Hall, recently demolished to make room for the new motorway,was said to be haunted. At any rate it was certified in 1518 that the ghost of James Parker had been seen some years before, and had given instructions that certain evidences were to be given to Joan and Janet, daughters of Hugh Banastre. The request was carried out and presumably James' troubled spirit was able to rest in peace.

The Parkers were connected with a number of well known families including the Chorleys. John Parker who died in 1610, married Alice Chorley at Chorley Church in November, 1593.

Their son and heir John Parker married Ann Nightingale and it was their initials I.P.A.P. that were cut in a datestone of the last Bagganley Hall, which they rebuilt in 1633.

John is thought to have been a warden at Chorley Church and to have signed the founding book of the old grammar school, in 1634.

The estate passed through the female line in 1788, to the Talbots, who give their name to the mill.

They in turn were succeeded by the Brethertons of Runshaw Hall.

GREAT FOREST

Much of the royal park supervised by the Parkers was forest. That could be the explanation for so many local names ending in "ley" which Professor Ekwall suggests could be from the Old English Lea—"glade, forest clearing". Thus Healey means a clearing on the slope of a hill—The Nab, obviously.

Knowley would be a similar space on a Knoll or little round hill. Little Knowley answers this description but Great Knowley further towards Blackburn seems rather large.

So far as the forest is concerned, if further proof were needed, it is provided by the Eaves in Eaves Lane. It stands for Old English "border of wood."

The Nab at eventide, viewed from the brook, where a footbridge crosses.

Botany Brow before the Motorway. Now only the Post Office on the left remains.

Canon Porteus using the theory of names, suggests that there was a great stretch of wood from Leyland to Bolton-le-Moors. He also suggests that the four Burgrages of Healey, were Hall-i'-th'-Wood, Higher Healey, Grey Heights and White House.

They would be occupied by tenants who would pay only a small rental in return because of their watching and warding.

Today there are parts of the valley which tell of past grandeur, not of parks and of glades so much as industry.

The canal which brought so many mills and factories also provided Chorley with a port at Knowley Wharf. Where the Botany Bay came from is a mystery. Most likely it was a nickname at first.

It was from here according to all advertisement in 1824 that boats left daily for Blackburn, Manchester, Liverpool and Leeds – for passengers as well as goods. Much of the property in the neighbourhood including a number of inns, was built on this account.

Some of the cottages which still seem to hang perilously on Knowley Top, were probably for bargees.

The reason why Eaves Lane itself is so broad and straight may have been to provide the link with the port.

In the first half of the last century, buildings on Eaves Lane were few. Apart from the stone cottages at each end, there was only Moss Cottage, Stump Mill and the workhouse.

Even when I came to Chorley the presence of the workhouse caused people to speak of Eaves Lane with hushed voices. The name was changed to the Institution, but the stigma lingered and anyone who died there was said to be buried from a number in Eaves Lane.

Yet when I first visited this place to report the Guardians Committee the view of the valley filled me with awe. It was not the bleak moorland scene I had expected but something infinitely more splendid.

Later I was to discover it was Chorley's hiking country, and to follow tracks that have led for centuries over the heights.

Not that I profess to know it that well. It is a place of many varieties, many moods. People who have lived there for years still keep finding something fresh, something new.

But the time to see it is just before sunset, standing by the bridge over the river nodoby owns – and there you sense its vastness, that here was a hunting place of kings!

nobody

CHAPTER SIXTEEN
LOVELIEST AND BEST LOVED

Upstream from the bridge that bears its name, the River Yarrow meanders down a valley so deep and well wooded, it is unseen by thousands who pass by daily on the trunk road only a few yards away.

It is for those who go by way of Three Steps and follow the footpath to the canal and the hills beyond, to discover the beauty of this corner of Duxbury, where the hum of the traffic mingles with the song of the birds.

On the other side of the valley is the canal, then railway so that within a space of less than half a mile, the Yarrow has company of three kinds of transport. Yet even that does not mar its beauty.

Between the railway and the canal, smoke drifts lazily from an old stone cottage, half hidden by the hedges and other growth. This bears the name Ridding, probably derived from a family who held land in these parts in ancient times. Roger de Ridings was mentioned as early as 1304, making a claim for common pasture against Henry, Lord of Duxbury.

Moving south along the towpath, past Winstanley Bridge the rush of water is heard and over a parapet one sees deep down, the river issuing forth. Those who thought Crosse Hall was Chorley's only aqueduct, are mistaken. There's one here!

The sharp turn has also taken the river under the railway, through a bridge concealed like the aqueduct by trees.

It is such a winding river this Yarrow, that it is hard to believe it is the same stream that comes down from Limbrick, which is nearly as far north as Yarrow Bridge. Yet it's here plain enough to see from the footpath that leads to Long Lane. This is the path that passes Old Joseph's Delph and Holland Fold.

Who old Joseph was is a matter of conjecture, but it was a sizeable quarry. It must have provided sandstone for many buildings round about and perhaps the canal bridges and bankings.

It was certainly in use before the railway because a tunnel was provided in the railway embankment through which the stone could be wheeled to the canal on bogies. The tunnel was hardly big enough for a horse, so the bogies must have been pushed by hand. But then, there was plenty of labour in those days.

The footpaths turns into a road at Holland Fold, and makes one wonder if perhaps it wasn't once a road all the way. The red roofed cottages in Long Lane, are still called by some "Travellers Rest" after an inn that was there, and inns are frequently at crossroads.

The railway and the canal run side by side at Duxbury and beneath both flows the Yarrow. One bridge can just be seen on the railway embankment on the right.

In this case, the other junction would be Hut Lane, which becomes a footpath, before emerging in Back Lane, near a barn that was once the parochial school for the mining families in the district. How it came to be called Abyssinia is a mystery, unless it was because the miners had black faces.

From the parochial School to the Yew Tree Inn is but a hop, skip and jump, and there you can see Nick Hilton's Bridge in the bottom, and it may surprise you to know that the stream flowing beneath it is the Yarrow again! It is in fact compensation water from a great bywash near the Rivington end of the Street out of the Rivington Reservoir.

From that you will gather it has not quite followed it's normal course all the way. Well is hasn't.

The old course made a horseshoe, the east side of which formed a deep valley the full length of the Street, the curve being about where the Rivington embankment is now.

There were houses and cottages on the river side, and at Street Bottoms a footpath that led to Street Wood on the Rivington side, crossed the river by a footbridge. Near to Street Bottoms there was also a weir, probably for the mill.

All that now presumably, lies under the water, along with the original mansion known as the Street.

The powers to build the reservoirs were obtained in 1847 but it was not until 10 years later that the Rivington Pike Scheme, as it was called was completed.

Rivington Reservoirs, started in 1852, was completed six years later at a cost of £900,000. Wages paid were in the region of a 1/- a day for a man and a 1/- a week for a boy.

FIRST CUSTOMER

The small reservoir at High Bullough (below Manor House) was acquired in 1856 from the small private company, who then supplied Chorley with water. Thus Chorley became one of the first customers of Liverpool Corporation.

The Pike Scheme extended to Tockholes, where the reservoir was connected by a canal called the Goit.

In 1865 an additional reservoir was built at Withnell, but even that was not enough for the thirst which had to be met by Liverpool Corporation. The Douglas and the Roddlesworth had been impounded. Now it was the Yarrow's turn, so a hundred years ago, Liverpool Corporation sought powers to dam up the Yarrow east of Anglezarke.

The work began a year later in 1868, and is of special interest, because if it is not the largest, Yarrow is certainly the deepest of the reservoirs.

The embankment which can be seen from Lister Mill Quarries and beyond, is 103ft. above the bottom of the dam. It is actually bigger than that if account is taken of the fact that the engineers had to dig more than 150 feet to reach a solid foundation.

In the deep trench cut across the valley, a wall was built in layers of nine inches deep. This was consolidated on both sides with earth from which all peat and unsound materials had been removed. The importance of the clay was inproviding a seal for the water.

Part of the 103ft. high embankment of Yarrow Reservoir. The tunnel through which water is fed into Anglezarke Reservoir was cut through the solid rock of the hill on the right.

QUARRY VILLAGE

The pitching on the water slopes and bed, is of millstone and this fortunately was in plentiful supply at Lister Mill Quarry nearby.

During the building of the reservoir, in fact, the base of the quarry became a village with its pub called the Clog, its blacksmith's shop and many cottages.

Much of the labour was Irish and one Irish foreman was particularly detested, it is said. When the job was nearing completion, a workman swore to leave something to remember the hated foreman by. He carved a face in a stone, which is still in one of the walls,

Looking down from the top of the embankment, on to the Anglezarke Reservoir. Lister Mill Quarry is on the right and across the lake is the hill alongside which runs the path from Haydock Fold (off Back Lane) to Knowsley Embankment.

TUNNEL THROUGH ROCK

Considering that the workers had little more than picks and shovels, it was a remarkable achievement that this reservoir should be completed in under ten years.

Apart from the embankment—a massive job in itself—there was an outlet bored through the rock of the hill into which part of the embankment is keyed. This enables water from the Yarrow to enter Anglezarke at control of a valve in the valvehouse at the top of the embankment.

There was also the popularly known as "The Waterfall," down which the overflow cascades into Anglezarke reservoir.

As all the reservoirs are interconnected, and as there is a bywash from Anglezarke to Rivington, some Yarrow water must find its way into the bywash past Cunliffe's.

But the old valley is now a lake, a pretty one albeit right as far as Allance Bridge. This seems to have cost the areas some beauty spots and pleasant walks, but it has provided others.

Reservoir buildings has been treated with respect through the ages. The second book of Chronicles honours Hezekiah, not only because he defeated Sennacherib by stopping up water supplies to his armies, but because he "also stopped up the upper spring waters of Gihon and brought them straight down on the west side of the City of David" (11 Chron 32-30).

The Liverpool Corporation may have dammed a beautiful valley, but there have been compensations besides water. At least the moorland country has been presented and many some day be recognised as a national park.

The original valley of the Yarrow can still be seen at Allance Bridge where from deep clefts in the rock, the Yarrow cascades from the hills to be joined by Limestone Clough, the stream which has rushed through Lead Mine Valley to meet it.

Another view from the top, this time showing Yarrow Reservoir. In the distance is Allance Bridge and beyond is Spitler's Edge. The weir at the front is the top of "The Waterfall."

134

It is a curious thing about the River Yarrow. It's name which means "The River" has remained unchanged through the centuries, and it still flows happily in a deep valley through woods and pleasant fields.

By some miracle, industry, highways, railways and canals have failed to spoil it. May it ever be so. It is not only the loveliest, but the best loved of our valleys.

At the head of the reservoir, the 'Meeting of the Waters', where the Yarrow (right) joins the Limestone Clough (left).

The tunnel in the hillside, through which waters flows from Yarrow to Anglezarke reservoirs.

A workman on the reservoir is said to have carved this stone in the likeness of an Irish foreman. It is part of the wall near Yarrow Reservoir.

CHAPTER SEVENTEEN

THE BLACK RIVER

Winter Hill, where the River Douglas has its source, can be seen from most places along its winding route to the sea. The T.V. mast may be said to mark the spot, for it is within twenty yards of Douglas Springs.

It was necessary to dig eight feet or more through the peat bog to reach solid ground before the mast and buildings could be erected. The moss is soaked by the springs and even in the driest season there is a stream across the moor towards Rivington Pike which bobs up like a conning tower below this hill which is 1,498 feet high.

On clear, summer days it is a place of breathtaking views and at other times it is the weather that takes the breath away.

Gales sweep across the lonely road which crosses appropriately-named Wilders Moor.

It is hard to believe that this was the main route to Blackburn but near to the T.V. mast is Scotsman's Stump, an iron pillar which is a memorial to George Henderson, a Scottish traveller who was shot nearby on November 9th, 1838, on his way to meet a fellow countryman at the Black Dog at Belmont.

His friend, who went out to meet him, found him on the roadside, dying of a gunshot wound.

A man was subsequently tried for murder, and acquitted, but the inscription on the stump describes Henderson as murdered, and for years afterwards a Piper used to visit the desolate moor on the anniversary of his death, to play a solemn lament! It must have been an eerie sound in the mists of November.

A ROUGH ROAD

On February 27th, 1958, this bit of moor was the scene of another tragedy when 35 businessmen from the Isle of Man were killed when their aircraft crashed in a blizzard.

There is no need to climb Winter Hill to see the Douglas in its infancy. George's Lane, Horwich, joins a very rough road past the Pike which crosses the Douglas where it skirts Brown Hill. Wigan people particularly are amused to read the warning notice which describes the stream as "drinking water."

In fact, the Douglas helps to fill Rivington Reservoir below. A most impressive view of this is across the deep valley near Old Lord's Height not very far from the fireclay works at Horwich. After the descent from the hill the stream is less turbulent and does not cut so deep.

It looks little more than a brook as it crosses Lever Park behind an iron fence south of Rivington and Blackrod Grammar School.

From this point the river is diverted to the reservoir which it enters at Hamer's Creek. The straight stretch which is rather like a canal can be seen from Rivington Lane. The original stream meandered through what are now gardens on Lever Park Avenue and residents still dig up rounded stones that had been the river bed.

OLD ANDERTON HALL RUINS

The compensation water from the reservoir goes under the Bolton road near the Squirrel Hotel and the Douglas becomes a river again marking the boundary between Rivington and Anderton. It descends noisily over a weir of an old mill and passes the ruins of the old Anderton Hall. This should not be confused with the Anderton Hall nearer to Rivington, also in ruins but built at a much later date.

The water is still clean and fit to support fish life but across the fields near the M61 the river passes a paperworks and from then on it changes in colour and smell.

Flowing between the motorway of the seventies, the railway of the nineteenth century and the Blackrod bypass of the thirties the Douglas goes under Grimeford Lane, which is believed to be part of the old Roman road between Blackrod and Walton-le-Dale. The Romans probably used the ford which was in existence before the bridge. There is also supposed to have been the hospice of St. Anthony on the riverside and the legs carved on the pillar of the headless cross nearby are said to represent those of the saint.

The water is dark and murky and is not improved when the river has gone under the A6 at Adlington near the dyeworks. Here it is also crossed by the canal and the bridge of a disused railway – quite an impressive complex!

The valley is pleasant along Adlington Common where an overgrown lane opposite to the south lodge of what was once Adlington Hall leads to a ford and a footbridge at Blackrod Bottoms.

Some people call the Blackrod side Paddy's Rise, the name it was known by when motor trials were held there in 1939.

THE DEEP VALLEY

This track leads to a bridge over the canal at Sharrock's Farm and connects with old lanes to Blackrod and Arley.

The valley becomes deep again where the soil is sandy and it is not easy to reach except on foot. It can, however, be intercepted as it were, by various footpaths such as the one in Chorley Lane almost opposite the signpost to Platt Lane.

People who follow this route to Arley are surprised to encounter the reservoirs of the Ashton-in-Makerfield Water Board. From these, the views of the distant hills including the one where the Douglas has started are worthy of any lakeland.

The inevitable question is, how can a river so filthy be allowed to mix with drinking water? The short answer is that it doesn't.

When the reservoirs were built the river was enclosed in a tunnel which stretches from Arley Brook to the Water Board yard at Worthington. It is about two thirds of a mile long.

Arley Brook passes Arley Hall, the moated building now the clubhouse of Wigan Golf Club and once the home of the Standishes of Arley.

Not far away at Boar's Head, the inn which gave the district its name bears the owl and the rat which was the crest of the Standishes of Standish.

Industry came early to these parts because of the river. On the site of the present dyeworks was a watermill as far back as 1384 and in 1791 the water was found adequate for papermaking. In 1859 the mill was owned by the proprietor of The Morning Post. Further downstream is Jolly's Mill which was driven by a waterwheel.

No doubt the cluster of factories round Leyland Mill Lane owe their origin to the Douglas. The valley is deep and well wooded.

It is even more picturesque as it passes the plantations of Haigh Hall, now a public park. At the old hall lived Mabel Bradshaw who was penanced for marrying again during the lifetime of her outlawed husband though she had waited two years. She had to walk barefoot each week to the cross in Wigan Lane known as Mab's Cross, so the legend says.

Wigan Lane runs parallel to the Douglas hereabouts and higher up is another reminder of its history. In the Civil War in 1651 Roundhead Colonel Lillburne caught up with Lord Derby's force on its way to join the King and in the bloody battle that followed, dispersed the Royalists, many of whom fled over the Douglas to be cut down on the steep banks across the way, which have ever since been known as the Bloody Mountains.

The Tyldesley Monument marks the spot where Sir Thomas Tyldesley, one of the heroes of the Civil War, died after his horse was shot from under him.

It was not the first time there had been a battle on the banks of the Douglas near Wigan.

It is not necessary to go as far as Whitaker, the Manchester historian, who claimed that four battles of King Arthur were fought on the banks of the Douglas. 'Wig,' the first part of Wigan, is said to be Saxon for fight, and various remains were unearthered near to what is now Parson's Meadow.

From the Bloody Mountains which are within musket shot of Wigan Rugby Club the Douglas flows under Powell Street and Crompton Street through Scholes to Poolstock. It had been diverted somewhat for a railway which is now disused and the old bridge can still be seen in a wall near The Ritz.

The new gyratory system has brought the river back in the public eye so to speak, and one road has been christened River-way.

AMUSING TO STRANGERS

Strangers to Wigan are apt to find this amusing, but the local people are proud of their river, and one of the multi-storey flats on the new Shores, which has risen above the dust and brickbats of the old, is Douglas House.

Between the gas undertaking and the power station the Douglas goes under the canal and Chapel Lane, to emerge in Wallgate near the Bird i' th' Hand where a local garage proudly displays the name of the river.

This section of river reveals an amazing variety of industry and dispels once and for all the idea once widely held that Wigan was only famous for coal. Old weirs among giant mills, some now unhappily idle, show that the Douglas brought cotton to the town in early days.

West of Wallgate the river runs behind some backyards complete with 'Petties' to emerge triumphant at Robin Park.

By now I had come to expect surprises and this was the biggest. Here are acres and acres of playing fields I never suspected existed before. Above the forest of rugby posts can be discerned in the distance Haigh Hall and the ancient Parish Church of Wigan.

The rest of the journey to Martland Hall is not so impressive and we hurry through Crooke which has less of historical interest than its name suggests, to Shevington, one of the new villages which has grown up outside Wigan within easy reach of the motorway.

THE DOUGLAS VALLEY

At Gathurst there is an amazing complex of bridges where the motorway spans the valley of the Douglas and at the same time crosses the canal, the railway and the road. From Deane Locks on the canal near the Gathurst Golf Course the river takes us through fields and trees. It may be fancy, but the water seems cleaner in these surroundings.

If we cross the motorway along Mill Lane we shall pass Finch Mill Farm. Finch House, the home of Bishop Edward Dicconson, the Roman Catholic Bishop of Malla, whose memorial is in Standish Parish Church was demolished a couple of years ago. Mill Lane takes us to Appley Bridge country route through Wrightington to Parbold.

This part of the valley is of singular beauty including Parbold itself, somewhat disfigured by quarrying. The easy way to view it is to strike south from Appley Bridge and turn right along Holland Lees Lane, where a number of fine houses such as Priorswood Hall show that builders of bygone days liked to overlook this part of the valley.

Of course, another way to Parbold is across Fishponds from Shevington, or straight up Appley Lane from Appley Bridge to Dangerous Corner. The Wrightington Hospital now occupies what was once the home of the Dicconson family.

It is not surprising to find that the hotel at Dangerous Corner carries their name, and what is even more interesting carries their arms in stained glass. Incorporated are four hinds heads. This explains why a number of hotels have that name in these parts for the Dicconsons were considerable landowners.

If we cross the main road at Dangerous Corner up Robin Hood Lane, we come to another hotel bearing the name of a famous local family but unfortunately, not the arms. The Rigbyes were lords of Harrock for many generations and one of their sons was Saint John Rigbye, canonised a short time ago.

From Parbold there are many views besides the one of Ashurst Beacon across the Douglas. There are also many footpaths and the hiker gets to know the river better than the motorist.

One of the places reached is the site of the old Douglas Chapel, now marked by a cross.

Jonathan Schofield who was curate at this chapel in 1662 was expelled on St. Bartholomew's Day for refusing to accept the Prayer Book. He is understood to have sheltered in South Tunley Hall, the home of the Wilsons who helped with the building of Tunley Presbyterian Chapel in 1691.

From Parbold the Douglas flows along open country between Hoscar Moss and Bispham. At one time it would have been crossed quite frequently by people going to and from Lathom House, the home of the Earls of Derby, which was demolished by the Roundheads after a second seige in the Civil War.

LEGEND OF THE EYRIE

It is not surprising to find at Bispham Green that the pub is called the Eagle and Child after the legend that when the lord of Lathom was without a male heir he left at the foot of a tree in which there was an eagle's eyrie a son born to him by a 'highborn maiden' not his wife.

The wife is said to have adopted the child on the assumption that it was brought by the eagle with Divine purpose.

The Douglas continues through the flat lands with Mawdesley and Croston on the east and Rufford on the west. At one time most of this area was under water with Rufford Old Hall and park standing out as high ground though nowhere reaching fifty feet above sea level.

The reason for this is that Marton Mere, a vast lake touching the manors of Scarisbrick, Burscough, North Meols, Tarleton and Rufford, drained into the Douglas.

In fact at one time most of the Douglas catchment area was called Lineas – the lake – and the Douglas or Asland was merely referred to as the river flowing through it. In 1692 Thomas Fleetwood of Bank obtained powers to drain the mere into the sea but after he died his gates were washed away and it was left to Thomas Eccleston of Scarisbrick to tackle the job in 1781.

Even now there is constant battle to keep the lowlands clear of water and the Douglas, steeply banked, flows above the level of the fields.

In spite of the flooding there were some well-to-do families hereabouts, notably the Heskeths of Rufford Old Hall. One of these, Richard Hesketh, tried to persuade Ferdinando, the fifth Earl of Derby to assert his claim to the succession of Elizabeth I because of blood relationship.

In some trepidation Ferdinando informed the Queen who had Richard beheaded. Ferdinando himself died soon afterwards of a mysterious illness the symptoms of which are suggestive of poisoning.

Flowing into the Douglas at Croston is the River Yarrow which itself is joined half a mile upstream by the River Lostock. These two rivers are deeply banked and tell their own tale of the fight against flooding in both Croston and Bretherton.

North of Rufford the Tarleton Ridge joins Hesketh Bank which forms the west bank of the Douglas to its estuary with the Ribble. In fact, until the Ribble Navigation Company reclaimed the northern part of the estuary in 1834 Hesketh Bank was a seaside resort. It was noted for its bathing, its salmon and its flounders.

Today it is a highly populated area and provides the only place that looks like a port on the Douglas.

NUMEROUS JETTIES

Behind the Becconsall Chapel built in 1764 (Becconsall was the dominant name in the area until 1718) the scene resembles something from W. W. Jacobs. There are numerous jetties and boats of all sizes whose masts point heavenwards or at 45 degrees dependent on whether the tide is in or out. Unfortunately there is mud where there must have been sand.

Yet as early as 1720 the River Douglas (alias Asland) Navigation Act was passed after nine years of preparation. Ultimately a waterway to Wigan was accomplished in 1774 by the Leeds–Liverpool Canal Company who acquired in 1783 the Douglas Navigation scheme. The canal and the river run very close together, in fact, most of the way from Blackrod, and nowhere closer than when they go under the road at Tarleton.

On the other bank of the Douglas are Little Hoole and Much Hoole, divided by a brook. Hoole Church, which according to tradition goes back to the 13th century but according to the datestone over the door was built in 1628 is chiefly famous for one of its curates, Jeremiah Horrocks, who on November 24th, 1639, observed the transit of Venus, from Carr House at Bretherton between performing his duties at afternoon service and sunset at 3.50 pm. He is generally regarded as the father of British astronomy.

The Horrocks Chapel was built as a memorial to him in 1857 and two years later a clock was added to the tower which already had a sundial.

THE IMPRESSIVE DOUGLAS ESTUARY

Extending along the east bank of the Douglas to the Ribble is a marsh which made Longton a popular resort in the days of the waggonette. From the Dolphin In it was possible to get a guide across the Douglas to Hesketh Bank.

Hesketh Bank itself provided a crosssing of the Ribble to Guides House on the other bank and there is no doubt that this route was used by Lord Derby in the Civil War when he went to raise men for the King in the Fylde where he had considerable possessions.

The estuary of the Douglas is quite impressive when viewed from the Freckleton side of the Ribble. It probably explains the name Asland, which applied to the lower course through the former vast lake called Lineas.

According to Professor Ekwall, Asland is old Norse, the first part coming from the word for ash trees, and the second part 'lone or 'lane'. To the Vikings the Douglas was a highway.

The name by which it was known upstream is British, from dubo, 'black' and glais, a 'stream.' Perhaps in the light of present day pollution it makes sense!